BOB BONTRAGER

EDITOR

# SEM

### and

# Institutional Success

INTEGRATING ENROLLMENT,
FINANCE *and* STUDENT ACCESS

SPONSORED BY SUNGARD® HIGHER EDUCATION

# SEM
and
# Institutional Success

American Association of Collegiate
Registrars and Admissions Officers
One Dupont Circle, NW, Suite 520
Washington, DC 20036–1135

Tel: (202) 293–9161 | Fax: (202) 872–8857 | www.aacrao.org

For a complete listing of AACRAO publications, visit www.aacrao.org/publications.

The American Association of Collegiate Registrars and Admissions Officers, founded
in 1910, is a nonprofit, voluntary, professional association of more than 10,000 higher
education administrators who represent more than 2,600 institutions and agencies in the
United States and in twenty-eight countries around the world. The mission of the Association is to provide leadership in policy initiation, interpretation, and implementation
in the global educational community. This is accomplished through the identification
and promotion of standards and best practices in enrollment management, information
technology, instructional management, and student services.

## LIBRARY OF CONGRESS CATALOGING-IN-PUBLICATION DATA

SEM and institutional success: integrating enrollment, finance, and
    student access/edited by Bob Bontrager.

    p. cm.

 Includes bibliographical references.

ISBN 978-1-5785808-5-9

1.  Universities and colleges—United States—Business management.
2.  Universities and colleges—United States—Finance.
3.  College attendance—United States—Planning.

I.  Bontrager, Bob.
II.  Title: Strategic enrollment management and institutional success.

LB2341.93.U6S46 2008
378.1'060973—DC22

2008039168

# Contents

# About the Authors

**BOB BONTRAGER** is director of AACRAO Consulting and the AACRAO Strategic Enrollment Management Conference. He has nearly twenty-five years experience in enrollment management at all types of institutions, with particular expertise in strategic planning, recruitment, marketing, financial aid, institutional budget strategies, and transfer programs. Most recently at Oregon State University, Bob's leadership resulted in a 40 percent increase in enrollment, including increases in the academic and diversity profile of the student body. He teaches and advises master's and doctoral students as a faculty member in Oregon State's College of Education.

Bontrager has been instrumental in developing and implementing a number of innovative programs. These include Oregon State's Degree Partnership Program, which promotes student access and baccalaureate degree completion through joint admission and concurrent enrollment at OSU and community colleges. Bontrager also provided leadership in the use of noncognitive variables in admission and scholarship decisions, with Oregon State emerging as a national leader in using these variables to more accurately assess student potential and enhance retention.

Prior to joining Oregon State in 1994, Bontrager served as vice president for enrollment management at Eastern Mennonite University in Virginia and was assistant registrar at Arizona State University. He earned his master of counseling degree and EdD in educational leadership and policy studies at Arizona State University. He earned his bachelor's degree at Goshen College, Goshen, Indiana, where he currently serves on the Board of Trustees.

**GUILBERT BROWN** is a Phi Beta Kappa graduate of the University of Denver where he majored in political science and philosophy. He attended graduate school in philosophy before beginning a career in nonprofit and higher education administration with an emphasis on long-term institutional planning and enterprise data systems. His work has focused on using technology to advance new analytical paradigms in financial transparency, budgeting, and enrollment management. Gil has authored numerous articles and presented his work in workshops and at annual meetings of AACRAO, the National Association of College and University Business Officers (NACUBO), the Society for College and University Planning (SCUP), and other organizations. He currently serves as the director of budget and financial planning at George Mason University in Fairfax, VA and as a senior consultant for AACRAO Consulting.

**DON HOSSLER** is a professor of educational leadership and policy studies and director of the Project on Academic Success at Indiana University. He is also the coordinator of the higher education and student affairs graduate programs there. Hossler has served as the vice chancellor for enrollment services for Indiana University Bloomington and the associate vice president for enrollment services for the seven campuses of the Indiana University system, the executive associate dean for the School of Education, and chair of the Department of Educational Leadership and Policy Studies. His areas of specialization include college choice, student persistence, student financial aid policy, and enrollment management.

Hossler has consulted with more than forty-five colleges, universities, and related educational organizations, including The College Board, Educational Testing Services, the University of Cincinnati, the Inter-American University of Puerto Rico, the Pew Charitable Trust, the University of Missouri, Colorado State University, the University of Alabama, and the General Accounting Office of the United States Government. He has presented more than 130 scholarly papers and invited lectures and is the author, or co-author, of twelve books and monographs and more than sixty-five articles and book chapters. Hossler is currently directing funded projects of The College Board, the Lumina Foundation for Education, and the Spencer Foundation focusing on student success and persistence. He has received national awards for his research and scholarship from the American College Personnel Association and the National Association of Student Personnel Administrators.

# Introduction

American higher education faces unprecedented challenges. The broad and complex scope of demographic, social, economic, and competitive forces make this a time unlike others that have gone before. Most of the major analyses of higher education in recent years have concluded that the number of Americans attaining a higher education credential will need to increase dramatically, with the largest increase needed among lower-income and underprepared students who are least likely to get such an education now. If ever there was a need to shift paradigms in the delivery of higher education, this is it.

It is the central thesis of this book that strategic enrollment management (SEM) offers a useful and unique conceptual framework for meeting today's challenges at the institutional level. By promoting clarity of institutional mission from the perspective of student access and success, SEM provides a paradigm for cutting through the clutter of competing priorities to focus on what will best serve student needs and support their educational attainment. The resulting alignment of institutional mission, enrollment goals, targeted investments, and budget outcomes enables planning that is more strategic, in turn leading to improved outcomes for the institution as a whole, as well as individual departments. But the potential benefits of SEM extend beyond institutions themselves. Because it operates from a student-centric mindset and directly affects enrollment patterns, SEM can and does play an important role in promoting student access and success, thereby addressing issues that are pertinent to American education as a whole.

The practice of SEM is not without controversy. As SEM practice has emerged and evolved over the past thirty years, the profession has experienced the growing pains inherent to any new endeavor. There have been a variety of definitions and manifestations of SEM practice that have led to a muddled understanding of what SEM actually is. Some observers have noted negative consequences resulting from specific SEM tactics, leading to criticism of the very concept of SEM. The purposes of this book are to:

- Describe the current financial and enrollment challenges facing American higher education
- Provide a definition and context for current SEM practice
- Offer new perspectives on the interplay of SEM and institutional finance
- Provide a SEM planning model that will enable institutions to concurrently improve mission, enrollment, and financial outcomes
- Promote the use of SEM concepts to improve student access and success

Ultimately, this book is part of the ongoing dialogue regarding the opportunities and challenges that accrue to higher education in the United States. The authors welcome comments and suggestions as we collectively seek more effective ways of meeting the needs of the students we serve.

Bob Bontrager
Corvallis, Oregon
August 13, 2008

CHAPTER ONE
*by* DON HOSSLER

1

# The Public Policy Landscape
## Financing Higher Education in America

The genesis of the comprehensive practices that are now associated with enrollment management is often traced to the decline in traditional-age high school students that began in the late 1970s and continued through most of the 1980s. During this period many institutions were forced to redefine their missions, serve new markets such as adult students, adopt more aggressive admissions marketing and financial aid policies, and/or focus more on student retention for the first time. These were the precursors of a comprehensive approach to student enrollments that became what we now call strategic enrollment management (SEM) (Maguire 1976; Hossler 1984; Hossler and Bean 1990; Dolence 1995).

With respect to enrollment challenges, not-for-profit colleges and universities in the United States have never faced as challenging a time period as we are likely to see in the next twenty years. These challenges include an increasingly difficult financial environment, demographic shifts that will create serious concerns for many institutions, an increasingly competitive marketplace, and, if all of these were not already enough to give one pause, institutions of higher education also find themselves in a more contentious public policy environment. Each of these alone would be sufficient to create apprehension for university presidents and boards of trustees, but as a group these considerations form an even more daunting set of challenges. This complex set of issues and the role of enrollment managers in helping to shape institutional responses to these concerns are the focus of this book. Too often senior campus policy makers, trustees, and faculty governance groups fail to step back and carefully review in a comprehensive manner the forces that are shaping the enrollment, revenue, prestige, and diversity goals for their institutions. Too often decisions are made about new student admissions goals, desirable net revenue goals from tuition and fees, decisions for achieving desirable diversity and access targets, and retention and graduation goals in an iterative and uncoordinated manner.

The environment for public and private non-profit colleges and universities has become more competitive than ever. Institutions face growing competition from private institutions that are establishing new branch campuses, from public two- and four-year institutions that are more aggressively recruiting students, from online asynchronous courses and degree programs, and from for-profit private universities that are offering an increasingly large array of degree programs. Against this backdrop of increased competition for students, we also face a dramatic shift in the demographic composition of potential college students. While the percentage of high school graduates will increase in the next decade, a large proportion of this next generation will come from families who have immigrated more recently to the United States. They will come disproportionately from Latino families whose parents may not have graduated from high school and, in fact, may not have attended high school. Many of these students will come from low-income families and will be more likely to be underprepared for the academic rigors of postsecondary education. Thus the competition for college prepared students is likely to intensify the pressure on enrollment managers.

In the last two decades the field of strategic enrollment management has evolved into a sophisticated management function that is expected to play a pivotal role in assuring that every campus has a satisfactory number of new students and currently enrolled students to provide sufficient net revenue, that the characteristics of the enrolled student body help to advance both the prestige and rankings of the institution, and that the ethnic and socioeconomic diversity of the enrolled student body demonstrate a commitment to equity and social justice. Today the primary task of enrollment managers is to manage the nexus of revenue, prestige, and diversity at the institutions at which they serve. Given the practice of tuition discounting that is being used by both private and many public institutions, unless enrollment goals are established in a strategic and integrated manner, SEM practices and policies can have an adverse impact upon the amount of campus dollars available for faculty and staff salaries, library expenditures, technology investments, and facilities. The ability of enrollment managers to achieve carefully coordinated campus enrollment goals can also have an impact upon external measures of institutional quality and accountability. These measures are receiving mounting degrees of attention from state and federal policy makers and more indirectly through the impact of college rankings publications.

This chapter will examine the impact of the current financial environment, important demographic changes, the increasingly competitive postsecondary education marketplace, and a more complex public policy environment upon strategic enrollment management, student access, and institutional financial outcomes. From the outset of this work we note that our attention is centered primarily on non-elite private four-year institutions and public four-year institutions. Although elite private colleges and universities and a handful of the most selective public research universities will not be totally immune from the effects of these trends, because of their wealth, prestige, and strong market position this group of institutions will not be strongly affected. Most of our discussion will focus on the concerns of non-profit four-year institutions that range from moderately selective to open admissions, that do not have large endowments, and that are not ranked among the top research, comprehensive, or baccalaureate degree-granting colleges and universities. Some sections will also be relevant for community colleges. Indeed, in some cases we will speak with specificity about the enrollment management challenges they face; however, they are not a primary focal point of this book.

## A TURBULENT FINANCIAL CONTEXT

While we would not try to argue that the current financial context for not-for-profit colleges and universities is more difficult than *any* previous periods in the history of American higher education, it is nonetheless a thorny and complex environment. For much of the twentieth century public policy makers believed that society was the primary beneficiary of increasing numbers of U.S. citizens earning postsecondary educational degrees. This was reflected in the relatively high levels of state support for public institutions. However, this belief in the societal benefits of higher education has declined in the last thirty years. Many legislators in both state and federal government advocate for policies that suggest that the principal beneficiary of postsecondary education is the individual, and thus government entities should not be expected to provide large amounts of government support for students enrolled in postsecondary education. These trends are perhaps most evident for public institutions as they continue to face reductions in the level of support from the legislatures in which they reside. This trend, coupled with efforts in many states to constrain the rate of increases in tuition and fees, has produced difficult financial situations. The developments have led to the emergence of support for further privatization of higher education in the United States, evidenced by the decline in public support for postsecondary education and in public policies that have enhanced the rise of the for-profit institutions. This is a profound shift that will continue to exert a powerful impact upon non-profit higher education.

Among private non-profit colleges and universities the effects of the increasing emphasis on the private benefits of postsecondary education have not been as pronounced. Indeed, declines in state support for public institutions have led to tuition increases that have helped to narrow the gap in tuition and fees in these two sectors, thus modestly leveling the competitive playing field between public and private colleges and universities. However, societal concerns regarding the high levels of tuition and fees in the private sector continue to present a major problem for less well-known institutions. The most elite private universities now charge tuition, fees, and, in many cases, room and board in excess of forty-five thousand dollars per year. There is a growing sense that continued increases in costs will drive more potential students to choose lower cost public institutions. In addition, many of these lesser known private institutions also have relatively small endowments. Consequently, they are confronted with difficulty in passing cost increases on to students and the inability to rely on endowments to provide a cushion from the rising costs of salaries, energy, and health care.

In recent years the plight of public universities has been well publicized. Between 1980 and 2000, the percentage of state budgets funding postsecondary education fell from near 9 percent to approximately 7 percent (NEA n.d.). To further exacerbate these declines, the number of students enrolling in public institutions has been increasing in many states. For example, in states in the Southeastern part of the United States, between 2001 and 2005, funding per full-time equivalent student fell by 3.3 percent (SREB 2006). This reality has resulted in a situation where these campuses are being asked to educate more students with fewer resources. In response to declining state support, many public institutions have increased tuition. However, governors and state legislators are reluctant to acknowledge the "catch 22" situation in which they have placed public universities. They want to reduce state subsidies and restrain tuition increases, while simultaneously seeing increased quality. Recent events in Florida and New Jersey are a good examples of these countervailing pressures (Hebel 2006; Lewis 2007). In one year Florida public colleges and universities have gone from the possibility of being permitted to increase tuition and raise much needed revenue, to being told to "hold the line on tuition," and seeing state funding reduced or at least failing to keep up with the increased numbers of students enrolling.

Private institutions face their own concerns. Except for a small set of wealthy elite institutions, most private colleges and universities rely heavily upon tuition to cover expenses. Without large endowments or state support most private institutions have to charge high levels of tuition. Indeed, over the past decade the average tuition and fees, adjusted for inflation, increased $5,746 (37%) at private four-year colleges

(Hebel 2006). These costs can be significant barriers to many students and their parents and, as a result, many of these institutions lack deep pools of potential students to enroll (Zemsky and Massy 2005). Furthermore, each time tuition is raised, institutions risk the possibility of shrinking the size of an already small pool of potential students. To offset high tuition rates, less well-known private institutions often provide generous tuition discounts to many enrolled students. Baum and Lapovsky (2006) report that in 2004–05 the average tuition discount provided to students in the form of financial aid at private institutions was 33.5 percent and for some institutions was as high as 48 percent. These high discount rates leave small revenue margins to pay faculty and staff, and to reinvest in the physical plant. Simultaneously, most federal and state financial aid programs have remained stagnant and, as a result, private institutions have been unable to rely on the federal or state government to make private higher education more affordable for students and their families.

## GROWING COMPETITION

In addition to the difficult financial pressure that most not-for-profit four-year institutions experience, they also face more competition for students than any recent time in our history. This competition comes from the growing for-profit private sector, from other countries who are enrolling an increasingly larger share of international students (a pool of students that at one time had primarily been the domain of colleges and universities in the United States), and from community colleges. Breneman, Pusser, and Turner (2006) document the growth in enrollments at baccalaureate degree-granting for-profit institutions. The number of bachelor's degrees earned at proprietary institutions nearly doubled between 1970 and 2002. In some states, the total number of degrees at all levels awarded by for-profit institutions increased by more than 20 percent between 1995 and 2000 (Turner 2006). The effects of institutions like the University of Phoenix and De Vry Institute of Technology goes beyond simple enrollment growth. For-profit institutions typically offer degrees in fields that have lower instructional costs such as education, public administration, business, and engineering-related technologies. Non-profit institutions often use the lower cost of instruction in these programs to provide cross-subsidies for more expensive undergraduate programs in the sciences and health care as well as for undersubscribed programs deemed to be important such as archaeology, classics, or music. This is referred to as *creaming*. These practices put pressure on the ability of non-profit colleges and universities to continue to offer a selection of more expensive or undersubscribed degree programs.

In addition to for-profit universities, universities from Australia, Canada, and the European Union have become much more aggressive about recruiting international students, including students from the United States. Over the past decade Australia has seen the largest increases in international student enrollments. During 2005–06, as Table 1.1 indicates, international student enrollments were on the rise (ACE 2006).

**Table 1.1**

ENROLLMENT GROWTH PERCENTAGES
BY COUNTRY (2005–2006)

| Country | % |
| --- | --- |
| Australia | 42 |
| France | 81 |
| Germany | 46 |
| Japan | 108 |
| United Kingdom | 29 |
| United States | 17 |

Public institutions located in other countries often have several advantages when recruiting international students. First, because in most instances public institutions are funded by the federal government (or central government as opposed to fifty individual state governments), the governments of countries such as Australia, New Zealand, and Singapore often assist in overseas recruitment efforts. The central government of these countries often see public postsecondary education as a product that can attract foreign students and thus foreign investment; Parker (2007) notes that the Australian tertiary education system has become the fourth largest source of foreign revenue in the nation. Secondly, since 9/11 the United States has made it more difficult for international students to secure visas for study in the United States, causing them to turn to other countries.

Finally, community colleges are also creating increased competition for the four-year sector. Competition from community colleges is happening for several reasons. The two most important reasons are lower tuition costs and the increasing number of state legislatures that are legislating or strongly encouraging the establishment of policies that direct more students to community colleges. State legislatures are enacting transfer and articulation agreements between the two- and four-year institutions that make it more attractive for students to begin postsecondary education at a community college because of lower tuition and the assurance that courses will transfer to a degree program at a four-year institution. The incentives for legislators to favor community colleges are clear. Community colleges require fewer tax dollars because costs of instruction are lower, thus state policy makers can assure citizens that they are providing low-cost access to all students. In the state of Florida, for example, students who graduate with less than a B average from high school and who want to attend a public institution have to begin their postsecondary career at a community college. Massachusetts is considering legislation that would make attending a community college free to all state residents. Recently New Jersey passed a law requiring that, upon acceptance, an associate degree awarded by in-state community colleges must be fully transferable and count as the first two years toward a baccalaureate degree at any of the state's public institutions. In addition, many community colleges are offering honors programs and other types of curricular incentives to attract a greater share of college-bound high school graduates. These developments do not just make it difficult for public institutions; they can also place hardships on private colleges and universities. As starting at a community college becomes normative for more students, and as transfer and articulation agreements become more common, less selective private universities have no choice but to also adopt the same transfer and articulation agreements. If they do not, students may not only fail to start their careers at a private institution, they also may not transfer. Indeed, one of the long term risks to private colleges is that if more students become accustomed to paying the lower tuition rates of community colleges, fewer students may be willing to pay the higher tuition rates of private institutions at the time they transfer.

Another problem that both public and private four-year colleges and universities face as more and more students start at a community college is a loss of revenue for the courses in first and second year general education programs. At most institutions, courses are larger and less expensive to teach at the 100 and 200 course level. The revenue generated at these levels is typically used to subsidize the smaller class sizes and more expensive instruction of delivering courses in students' majors. Thus the loss of income from general education courses can place financial stress on four-year colleges and universities.

## DEMOGRAPHIC SHIFTS

In the midst of increased competition and complex financial issues, we also find ourselves in the midst of dramatic shifts in the size and composition of the high school population. Nationally, the number of students graduating from high school is projected to increase through 2008–09. By 2013–14 most states will see increases in the number of Hispanic high school graduates ranging from 50 percent to more than 200 percent (Western Interstate Commission on Higher Education 2003). These students are more likely to be first generation, low income, and from recent immigrant families (Hossler 2006). In addition, the number of white high school graduates is projected to decline; because they enroll in larger percentages than Hispanic students, this will probably lead to enrollment pressures for institutions of higher education. Hispanic students who do matriculate are more likely to need financial aid and are more likely to attend community colleges. Current policy trends juxtaposed with demographic trends raise interesting possibilities for the future of college admissions. Despite larger numbers of high school students, many institutions could struggle to achieve enrollment goals in many states. Competition for college-prepared students may intensify. Institutions with deep applicant pools may not experience enrollment declines, but the characteristics of the enrolled student body and thus the culture of the student body may undergo noticeable changes. The next two decades are likely to place significant pressures on enrollment managers.

## A CONTENTIOUS PUBLIC POLICY CONTEXT

If financial concerns and an increasingly competitive environment were not enough to deal with, public and private institutions also face the very real threat of a more intrusive public policy environment. For two decades at the federal level there has been growing concern about the tuition costs of colleges and universities. In 1997, Education Secretary Riley, under the auspices of President Clinton, created the National Commission on the Cost of Higher Education. The recommendations of many committees have focused on rising costs, the confusion about financial aid, and the actual costs most students and families pay for postsecondary education. The committee deliberated for several months and although the committee did not ultimately recommend legislative actions to constrain college costs, the report is critical of the upward spiraling costs of both private and public postsecondary education. Since that time a spate of reports have been published criticizing the rising tuition costs (Boehner and McKeon 2003; Lumina Foundation 2004).

In 2006–2007, many of the same issues were revisited when Margaret Spellings, the Secretary of Education, established a national commission (the "Spellings

Commission") to examine both the costs and the quality of our postsecondary educational system. It is premature to make any final judgments about the long-term impact of the Spellings Commission on federal policy. However, some identified themes in the final committee report were consistent with recurring concerns raised about postsecondary education in recent years. These include continued increases in college costs and the impact upon access for low-income students, a focus on the quality of postsecondary education and what students learn, and a focus on student persistence and academic success. Secretary Spellings made an unprecedented but unsuccessful effort to use federal power in coordinating the somewhat disparate accreditation processes used across the nation to advance her concerns about quality and graduation rates. These efforts attracted considerable attention and criticism as to the appropriate role of the federal government in regulating accreditation and, indirectly, measures of quality in postsecondary education. While this effort was unsuccessful, it is likely that federal and state policy makers will continue to advocate for the use of retention and graduation rates as indirect indicators of the quality of education. Although it failed, this effort indicates that the interest in postsecondary education quality is rising and that the attention being given to persistence and graduation rates is likely to increase because those rates can be easily measured.

In addition to the focus of the Commission on college quality, the chair of the Commission, Charles Miller, took the position that the costs of postsecondary education and the complex financial aid system that includes multiple federal, state, and institutional programs are broken. Charles Miller is not the only critic of the patchwork financial aid system in this country. The College Board launched a national *Commission on Re-Thinking Student Aid* to examine the problems with the federal and state financial aid systems. In addition, a spate of books has recently been published on the financial aid system. Collectively, these developments suggest significant concern about college costs and financial aid. Some legislators and policy analysts have called for major reforms to the financial aid system. Given the focus on costs and financial aid, it is possible that we will see such changes in the next few years.

Along with concerns about financial aid, there is renewed concern about access to admission and degree completion for low-income students. Low-income students, students who graduate high school at least minimally qualified, as defined by the U.S. Department of Education, enroll in four-year institutions at half the rate of comparably qualified high-income peers. In addition, only six percent of students from the lowest strata of socioeconomic status (SES) earn a bachelor's degree compared to 40 percent with the highest SES (Advisory Committee on Student Financial Assistance, February 2001), and students in the top third of the income distribution in the United States are more than seven times more likely to earn a college degree than students in the lowest third of income groups.

Concerns about persistence and graduation rates are not limited to four-year institutions. Community colleges are coming under increasing scrutiny about low degree attainment and transfer rates (Doyle 2006; Driscoll 2007). Those recent reports, along with the Lumina funded *Achieving the Dream Project* that focuses on efforts to enhance degree attainment in community colleges, demonstrate the increasing pressure on community colleges to improve persistence and transfer rates to baccalaureate degree-granting programs. Some studies suggest that as few as 20 percent of those students entering community colleges ever transfer (Wellman 2002). The national six-year graduation rate for students enrolled in a community college is 28.3 percent (Bailey, Jenkins, and Leinbach 2005). Some policy analysts believe that the increasing scrutiny focused on academic success at community colleges will become one of the most important public policy issues of the next decade (Voorhies, August 2007, personal conversation).

These concerns dovetail with many of the connections between quality and graduation rates raised by the Spellings Commission. Increasingly, public and educational policy makers suggest that the appropriate measure of access for low-income and disadvantaged students is not matriculation to a college or university, but rather, once admitted, the opportunity to persist to degree completion. In reply to these concerns, both federal and institutional policy makers have taken steps to increase access to higher education. In September of 2007 Congress used savings from reductions in subsidies to lenders to provide a significant increase in funding for Pell Grants. Several private and public universities have taken dramatic steps to increase access. Elite institutions such as Amherst and Princeton (Hoover 2007; Marklein 2004) have take proactive steps with financial aid to increase the number of low-income students enrolling. Many public institutions have also enacted financial aid policies to improve access to low-income students. Perhaps best known among these programs is the University of North Carolina Covenant Program and *Access UVA* at the University of Virginia. Both of these programs promise that any low-income students admitted will receive sufficient financial aid to earn a degree without the need for loans. This strategy is based on the belief that this will enhance matriculation and graduation rates for low-income and first-generation students.

## STRATEGIC ENROLLMENT MANAGEMENT AND UNCERTAINTY REDUCTION

Collectively, these issues create a complex web of pressures on enrollment managers. One of the expectations both boards of trustees and presidents have for senior administrators is uncertainty reduction. In the case of enrollment managers, they are looking for strategies and tactics that will balance the campus budget and assure the trustees that the campus will be considered at least as good or even better than the other institutions in their peer group of two-year or four-year institutions. They want to be certain that the campus reflects the ethnic and socioeconomic diversity of the region. These are difficult tasks in relatively stable environments. Current trends suggest that the next fifteen to twenty years will not be a period characterized by stability for enrollment managers.

However, the strategies, policies, and practices that have evolved and that have been employed by enrollment managers in the last twenty years can provide a data driven planning environment where thoughtful senior policy makers can still help to shape the size, quality, and diversity of enrolled student bodies. The same analytical tools used to increase the enrollment of high-ability students can be used to devise plans for increasing the ethnic diversity of a student body, or to increase the number of low-income students who persist until graduation. Such decisions require trade-offs, but they can be accomplished. These concerns and the role of SEM in finding solutions for campus policy makers are the focus of the remainder of this volume. In succeeding chapters we consider definitions of strategic enrollment management in order to provide a strong foundation for looking more carefully at SEM. Our focus on strategic enrollment management and institutional financing strategies also leads us to examine the factors that are influencing the costs of higher education in the United States. With this foundation, we move on to look at how strategic enrollment management and fiscal planning and budgeting should be integrated. Indeed, we argue that SEM cannot be successful if these two functions are not viewed in a holistic manner. Finally, we close with a chapter that synthesizes our thinking about strategic enrollment management, institutional finance, and public policy issues in higher education.

CHAPTER TWO
*by* BOB BONTRAGER

2

# A Definition and Context for Current SEM Practice

Strategic enrollment management (SEM) is often misunderstood as an enhanced approach to admissions, marketing, and financial aid. In fact, it is a far more complex approach to meeting the broad range of internal and external challenges referenced in Chapter 1; it requires fundamental changes in the way institutions think and act with regard to enrollment goals. Deployed effectively, SEM offers a conceptual framework for addressing enrollment challenges and broader strategic initiatives, including the seemingly disparate goals of access and robust financial outcomes for an institution. But more than a conceptual framework is needed. As Copeland and Wells (2008, p. 1) note, "the difference between a concept and a well-executed strategy can be vast."

The unique utility of SEM is its inherent link between concepts and processes. SEM enables institutions to fundamentally rethink their approach to achieving enrollment goals. More importantly, it is a driver for change in institutional practices and related outcome measures, in areas ranging from admission policy to service delivery to curriculum planning. By implementing such changes in their unique contexts, institutions can begin to shape an effective response to the many enrollment-related challenges currently facing American higher education.

This chapter will describe how this book defines and perceives SEM. In addition, it will further clarify the current context of SEM practice that underlies the discussion and suggested solutions in subsequent chapters.

## SEM DEFINED

There are many worthy definitions of strategic enrollment management. It is indicative of the breadth, complexity, and multi-perspective nature of SEM that a range of definitions exist. Kalsbeek (2006) summarizes these various perspectives on SEM into four "orientations."

The *administrative orientation* focuses on the coordination, integration—and, often, the co-location—of varied enrollment-related processes at an institution.

The *academic orientation* focuses on the development of curricula and academic support programs that provide relevant content and credentials; that are accessible in terms of time, location, and delivery mode; and that facilitate student persistence and educational goal attainment.

The *market-centered orientation* focuses on the institution's market position relative to other institutions of higher education, with the goal of ensuring competitiveness of its academic programs and elevating its position within its targeted audiences or markets.

The *student-focused orientation* focuses on caring for the students who benefit from or participate in enrollment-related processes and initiatives.

Achieving higher levels of coordination among these related but disparate orientations within an institution is the defining challenge of SEM. At the core of this challenge is the dynamic tension between institutional and student interests. The administrative, academic, and market-centered orientations each imply the implementation of activities that ultimately will address student needs. However, they run the risk of drifting from a focus on students to a focus on the interests of institutions or of governing bodies. Over time, administrative structures and processes may begin to reflect institutional/bureaucratic expediency more than effectiveness in meeting student needs. Curricular offerings often reflect the schedules desired by faculty, rather than what will be the most convenient time for students to attend a particular class. A market-centered orientation too often devolves into discussions of advertising tactics, rather than an understanding of market needs among both students and employers and how best to address them.

As referenced in this book, strategic enrollment management is defined as a *coordinated set of concepts and processes that enables fulfillment of institutional mission and students' educational goals* (Bontrager 2004). This definition brings together the disparate orientations to SEM and directly addresses the necessary juxtaposition of concept and process, as well as institutional and student interests. For example, many institutions focus on the *processes* of enrollment—such as admitting students, marketing the institution, dispersing financial aid, delivering academic advising, and so forth—without an overarching conceptual framework that allows these necessary enrollment processes to be aligned for maximum effectiveness in meeting student needs and, ultimately, enrollment goals. However, when institutions fail to achieve their enrollment goals, it is rarely due to a lack of attention to processes. Rather, the failure can usually be traced to an inadequate grasp of SEM *concepts*. Institutions often fail to recognize the inherent link between institutional mission and student goals. Among the core *concepts* of SEM is the notion that perhaps the clearest manifestation of institutional mission is the profile of the students enrolled at the institution. The profile of students refers to the mix of students from entry

## Table 2.1

### SAMPLE ENROLLMENT GOALS FOR A LAND-GRANT UNIVERSITY

| | Current | | 10-Year Targets | |
|---|---|---|---|---|
| | n | % | n | % |
| **Total Headcount** | 10,000 | | 12,000 | |
| **Student Level/Type** | | | | |
| *Undergraduate* | | | | |
| Campus-based | 8,500 | | 9,000 | |
| Distance Education | 500 | | 1,000 | |
| Undergraduate Total | 9,000 | 90.0 | 10,000 | 83.3 |
| *Graduate* | | | | |
| Campus-based | 750 | | 1,500 | |
| Distance Education | 250 | | 500 | |
| Graduate Total | 1,000 | 10.0 | 2,000 | 16.7 |
| **Undergraduate Demographics** | | | | |
| *Geographic Origin* | | | | |
| In-State | 8,000 | 88.9 | 8,500 | 70.8 |
| Other States | 900 | 10.0 | 1,300 | 10.8 |
| International | 100 | 1.1 | 200 | 1.7 |
| *Race/Ethnicity* (targets based on state population trends) | | | | |
| African American | 150 | 1.7 | 350 | 3.5 |
| Asian/Pacific Islander | 700 | 7.8 | 800 | 8.0 |
| Caucasian | 7,725 | 85.8 | 7,650 | 76.5 |
| Hispanic | 300 | 3.3 | 1,000 | 10.0 |
| Native American | 125 | 1.4 | 200 | 2.0 |

until graduation or goal attainment, thus providing a direct measure of student satisfaction and success.

This is not to say that student profile is the only manifestation of institutional mission, nor is it the only important one. All the elements of teaching, research, and service are critical to the ultimate success of any college or university. However, it is difficult to imagine a more powerful reflection of an institution's raison d'être than the number and types of students it enrolls. SEM can serve as an organizing construct to bring greater clarity to institutional mission, thereby enabling fulfillment of the mission itself, as well as an institution's enrollment goals.

Crafting detailed, mission-based enrollment goals leads to compelling strategic planning conversations. Table 2.1, on page 19, gives a basic example of what enrollment goals might look like for a land-grant university that seeks to:

- Increase overall enrollment;
- Increase the proportion of graduate enrollment to reflect the profile of peer institutions;
- Increase nonresident and international students to bolster revenue and enhance students' educational experience; and
- Increase ethnic diversity to better fulfill the university's land-grant mission and enhance students' educational experience.

The questions raised in developing goals at this level of detail are many. What are the appropriate mission-based student categories that need to be tracked? What are the "right" proportions of students in the categories identified? Which of these categories is highest priority and will be addressed first as annual incremental targets are established?

At first glance it may seem that answering these questions is relatively easy, at least among the major categories of institutions. A public land-grant university presumably will devote more attention to enrolling in-state students, whereas the sister "flagship" campus will enroll more nonresident students. Smaller private institutions, except for those with explicit national reach, will generally seek to attract and retain students who live in nearby communities or neighboring states. Community colleges will provide transfer, vocational/professional, technical, and continuing education certificates and two-year degrees to students in their local service districts.

Yet we find institutions of all types experiencing "mission creep" due to an array of factors. Those factors may include financial pressures or pursuing a perceived avenue to enhanced prestige. As a result, a land-grant university may seek to enroll greater numbers of nonresident, higher-paying students. Private colleges may try to extend their reach geographically in an attempt to enroll additional students from new target markets. And, in recent years, a growing number of community colleges have added four-year degree programs as a means of increasing enrollment (Fliegler 2006).

Indeed, developing the detailed enrollment goals required to drive SEM is a complex and time-consuming undertaking, leading many institutions to avoid the process entirely. As a result, they experience confusion related to their goals, deliver recruitment and retention programs that lack focus, and find themselves continually underperforming with regard to desired enrollment outcomes.

In our quest to reach numerical enrollment targets, we dare not lose track of the fact that we are talking about students. Institutions of higher education are tempted to assume that the altruistic underpinnings of education themselves make a student focus "understood." Indeed, those of us who choose to work in higher education have a nearly uniform passion for assisting students in achieving their educational goals. Nonetheless, we carry out the educational enterprise as human beings operating within bureaucratic organizations. Our better intentions notwithstanding, competing interests from the full range of campus stakeholders can come to the fore at any given time, and distract us from our institutional mission and our students' best interests.

The particular approach to SEM advocated here posits that effective recruitment and retention programs, at the most basic level, rely on meeting students' needs and aspirations in a timely way. This includes every aspect of the student experience, from curriculum to enrollment services to student life programs. While this has been the conceptual key to SEM since its emergence as a large-scale enterprise in the 1980s, its implications become even more significant as the proportion of college students who are members of groups traditionally underserved by higher education grows. Colleges and universities face serious access and equity challenges as they seek to meet the needs of aspiring students who are increasingly diverse on a range of cultural, social, economic, and educational variables (Bontrager 2007).

## THE EVOLUTION OF SEM PRACTICE

The practice of strategic enrollment management emerged in the anticipation and impact of a demographic downturn that began in 1980. Prior to that time, higher education in the United States experienced nearly constant growth, from its inception with the establishment of Harvard College in 1636. Expansion of American higher education received a major boost with the 1862 Morrill Land Grant Act, perhaps the most visible by-product of a broad range of education initiatives at the local and state levels that occurred in the pre- and post-Civil War era (Thelin 2004). The Morrill Act "democratized" higher education by giving rise to affordable, practical alternatives to the options that existed for students prior to that time (p. 75).

This populist approach, and the enrollment growth that followed, accelerated even more rapidly from the 1950s through the 1970s, due to a succession of societal and demographic changes. From the G.I. Bill in the 1950s, to the Civil Rights movement in the 1960s, to the population bubble of the baby boom generation in the 1970s, higher education saw an expansion of interest and access that provided a steady stream of students. However, even when campuses were flush with students, and indeed throughout the history of higher education, colleges and universities have been concerned not only with enrollment itself, but also with the types of students they are able to attract. Campuses made efforts to more effectively recruit targeted groups of students through enhanced market segmentation, improved recruitment services, and merit aid well before the modern SEM era (Henderson 2001).

By the early 1970s, those who were carefully monitoring trends in higher education could see challenges looming as they noted an upcoming decline in high school graduates. This decrease in the number of students graduating from U.S. high schools began as the last members of the baby boom generation finished high school in the late 1970s. From that point through the mid-1990s, the number of high school graduates was in free-fall, dropping nationally by 700,000 students, over 20 percent, by 1995.[1]

The demographic shift varied among institutions and regions of the country. For many colleges and universities, the decrease in high school graduates was balanced through the 1980s by increases in the number of nontraditional students they enrolled, such as adult degree completers and students of color. Enrollment of these new groups allowed many institutions, especially public schools in urban locations, to maintain or even increase their enrollments. Institutions in the South and West were aided by population shifts to those regions, a population realignment that continues today.

Whatever the situation with local demographics, virtually every college and university found itself with a new set of tasks and expectations around institutional marketing. It was during this time that marketing higher education, previously considered anathema to the scholarly enterprise, came to the fore.

By the early 1990s the magnitude of the demographic downturn caught up with virtually every segment of higher education, with financial changes adding

---

[1] Historical data derived from various editions of NCES *Projections of Education Statistics*. See < http://nces.ed.gov/programs/projections/>.

an additional burden. While strategic enrollment management emerged initially in response to demographics, it gained prominence in an environment of two financially-related factors: increased accountability and constrained resources. Criticism of the rapid rise in college tuition costs, which began during this period and continues today, is especially relevant to the SEM enterprise. In knee-jerk, short-sighted efforts, many institutions have fallen into the trap of throwing money at their enrollment problems, with too little planning and a lack of accountability for achieving the desired outcomes.

At the same time, another economic force has become increasingly challenging. Much of this phenomenon can be traced to the dramatic decline in public support for higher education, especially from the states. Reflecting a series of public policy choices since 1980, the share of higher education financing assumed by students and families has grown dramatically. This trend continues today with public higher education having "grown less public and more private," and students having been left to pay a larger share of their educational costs (Mortensen 2008, p. 13). Private institutions feel the pinch as well, particularly in states with programs that provide financial assistance to students attending private institutions, where funds also have been cut.

In this environment, colleges and universities began to employ more comprehensive approaches to enrollment, which moved beyond recruitment and marketing programs to include sophisticated financial aid strategies, institutional research, and retention efforts. Thus, by the mid-1990s, strategic enrollment management began to be viewed by many institutions as resource management.

In addition to traditional recruitment and retention strategies, enrollment managers have expanded their tool kits to include "efficiency" strategies such as geo-demographic research, financial aid leveraging, information management, and a broadening array of educational outcomes assessments. These tools and many others are woven together into comprehensive, long-term enrollment programs that often are as much about using resources efficiently as they are about achieving enrollment goals. Indeed, these tools have developed and gained prominence as primary contributors to the SEM movement.

## ENVIRONMENTAL CHALLENGES

The current context in which SEM practitioners operate is changing again in ways that will forever alter how we do business as institutions of higher education. That

**Figure 2.1** ▸

U.S. High School
Graduates,
1994 to 2022

**SOURCE**: WICHE, 2008

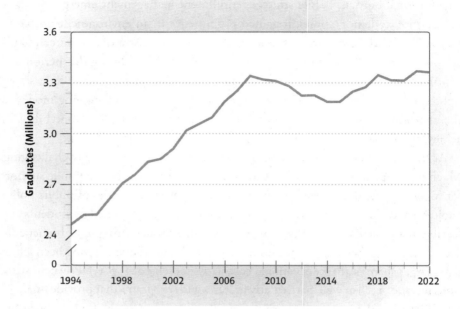

context is made up of new or newly-evolving challenges related to the same environmental factors that have influenced the emergence of SEM from the beginning: demographics, economics, and institutional priorities. These issues have gained increased attention as observers contemplate the significant implications for the practice of SEM, institutional outcomes, and the long-term economic and social well-being of the United States (Bontrager 2007; Green 2004; Kalsbeek 2005; Whiteside 2003).

### Demographic Factors

According to the Western Interstate Commission for Higher Education (WICHE 2008), the number of high school graduates in the United States has increased since 1994, an upward trend that will continue through at least 2022 (see Figure 2.1).

While there will be decreases in the next several years before the number goes up again, the number of graduates will remain at least on par with 2005, which saw a 30 percent increase over 1994. This would seem to bode well for enrollment managers. However, the aggregate numbers mask stark realities. The current demographic environment is splitting regions and broad cohorts of the American public into

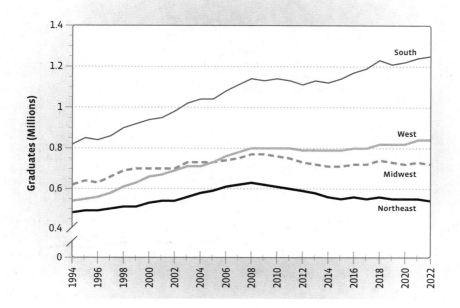

◄ **Figure 2.2**

U.S. High School
Graduates,
by Region,
1994 to 2022

**SOURCE:** WICHE, 2008

"haves" and "have-nots." As demonstrated in Figure 2.2, states in the South and West will see large increases in the number of public high school graduates, while states in the Northeast and Midwest will see numbers decline (WICHE 2008).

These geographic changes are even more striking from the perspective of the racial/ethnic composition of high school graduates. It has been well documented that the U.S. is becoming more diverse; this is also true of high school graduates nationally, as illustrated in Figure 2.3, on page 26 (WICHE 2008).

The implications of these demographic shifts are daunting enough, given higher education's modest gains in bachelor's degree completion rates among underrepresented students. There have always been wide gaps in educational attainment among racial/ethnic groups, and they are getting wider. From 1980 to 2000, bachelor's degree attainment increased for persons aged 25 to 64 in each of the major racial/ethnic groups. However, the increase was significantly greater for white and Asian-American students. In 2000, whites aged 25 to 64 were twice as likely as African Americans to have a bachelor's degree and almost three times as likely as Hispanics/Latinos (National Center for Public Policy and Higher Education 2005).

**Figure 2.3** ▶

Cumulative
Percent Change
in U.S. Public High
School Graduates
by Race/Ethnicity,
2005 to 2022

**SOURCE:** WICHE, 2008

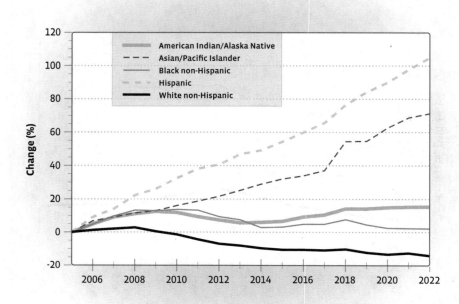

*Economics*

These demographic changes become even more challenging when cross-referenced with the confounding economic forces at play in the current environment, namely rising costs, declining state support, and the increasing financial need of students seeking access to higher education. These factors have been reported repeatedly in higher education literature and will not be reviewed at length here, except to highlight the important relationship between racial/ethnic diversity and family income. As Figure 2.4 (on page 27) illustrates, median family income varies significantly among the major racial/ethnic groups.

Anyone who values diversity and equity will be concerned about these data. For educators, they take on added meaning when considered in light of the relationship between family income and bachelor's degree attainment. Additional data compiled by Mortensen (2006) indicate that persons from the top quartile of family income in the United States are nearly six times more likely to earn a bachelor's degree than persons from the lowest quartile. Among the latter group, only about 12 percent earn a bachelor's degree by age twenty-four (see Figure 2.5, on page 28).

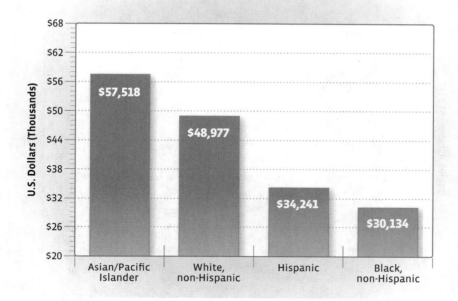

◄ **Figure 2.4**

U.S. Median
incomes, 2004

**SOURCE:** U.S.
CENSUS BUREAU

These demographic and economic trends present enormous challenges to higher education leaders as they seek to effectively manage their institutions. The inherent difficulty in effectively addressing those challenges is reflected in the call for improved performance measures and accountability. A Lumina Foundation report cites the need to demonstrate accountability that extends beyond basic numbers to address institutional purposes and high-quality outcomes (Dickeson 2004).

Critics of higher education, and of strategic enrollment management in particular, often fail to grasp the complexity of that context. A superficial analysis invites some to conclude that SEM and its practitioners are the source of the problem (Haycock 2006). In fact, with its comprehensive approach to enrollment, SEM offers one of the few avenues for achieving the goals of access and equity for students, while maintaining viable financial outcomes for institutions.

## THE FINANCIAL DYNAMICS OF SEM

Strategic enrollment management is generally linked with two finance-related activities: financial aid leveraging and net revenue strategies. Financial aid leveraging,

**Figure 2.5** ▶

Estimated
Baccalaureate
Degree Attainment
by Age 24 by
Family Income
Quartile, 2005

**SOURCE**: POSTSECONDARY
EDUCATIONAL
OPPORTUNITY, 2006

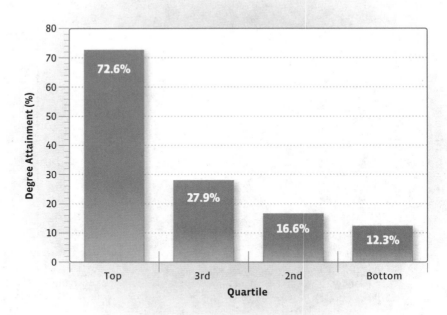

alternatively referred to as tuition discounting, is the practice of allocating varying amounts of discretionary financial assistance to admitted students based on a range of student characteristics and circumstances. Institutions analyze this information to determine a given student's eagerness to attend and corresponding willingness to pay, and subsequently adjust financial aid packages to students accordingly.

The practice of financial aid leveraging is perhaps the most prominent strategy used to increase an institution's net revenue, but it is not the only one. The most robust deployments of SEM include return on investment—or net revenue—as an explicit outcome of virtually every recruitment and retention initiative they pursue. Viewing SEM in this way is a core concept of this book and the basis of the remaining chapters.

Because factors other than just financial need are considered, a leveraging strategy will result in instances in which some students with greater financial means will receive a more favorable financial aid package than other students with lesser financial means. Observers from outside the SEM profession have decried the practice of financial aid leveraging and the pursuit of net revenue, often equating negative leveraging/revenue practices with the whole of SEM. One such report unfavorably characterizes enrollment management as institutions "[using] their resources to compete with each other for high-end, high-scoring students instead of providing a chance for college-qualified students from low-income families who cannot attend college without adequate financial support" (Haycock 2006, p. 2).

Such criticisms can certainly be accurate in some instances. Often, however, the issues are more complicated. Low- to moderately-priced institutions that lack large endowments are typically required to offer non-need based aid (or merit aid) in order to attract more academically capable and more affluent students to enroll. In doing so, some colleges and universities are able to generate sufficient net revenue to invest more money in need-based aid. Additionally, merit aid helps to meet need for some students. However, in these instances it behooves enrollment managers to be honest with themselves and their presidents, keeping track of how much merit-based financial aid is actually meeting student need.

These same leveraging tools are often used to increase diversity or to increase the number of students with "special talents" such as music, drama, athletics, or student leadership. The temptation to focus excessive amounts of aid on these target cohorts of students is real. Indeed, it may happen too frequently that too much financial aid ends up going to affluent students and too little to needy students. This is most likely to occur in the special talent areas, since they to correlate strongly with wealth-enabled opportunities.

However, broad critiques too often miss the nuances and complexities of these situations. Some public institutions may be mandated by their state legislatures or coordinating boards to increase the quality, diversity, or special talents among the students enrolled. Both public and private institutions may face these kinds of mandates from their Boards of Trustees. This is not to suggest that SEM practitioners are absolved of responsibility for addressing inequities in higher education's enrollment patterns. At the same time, it seems inappropriate to single out enrollment managers as culprits in perpetrating undesirable outcomes that actually result from a much broader range of goals and decisions at both the public policy and institutional levels.

SEM critiques tend to further oversimplify the situation by focusing on just one of SEM's many potential tactics—that is—basing financial aid decisions on willingness to pay. When this tactic is used, it rarely is deployed in isolation. Rather, it is generally used in the context of a complex matrix of strategies and tactics designed to meet the full range of institutional enrollment goals. A case can be made that it is appropriate to employ this tactic as a part of a broader SEM plan, based on the rationale that the educational experience for all students on a given campus is enhanced by having a critical mass of high-ability students. Most institutions legitimately seek to enroll their fair share of the "best and brightest" persons from the student populations they serve. Indeed, this aspect of an institution's enrollment plan usually receives the most attention and support among the campus faculty.

It should also be noted that when financial aid leveraging is used, SEM practitioners regularly advocate the use of financial need as a leveraging variable, thereby expressly shifting funds from less needy students to those with greater financial need. Moreover, most enrollment managers will seek to balance efforts targeted toward higher-ability and higher-income students with other initiatives aimed to enhance access and equity.

## SUMMARY

The central thesis of this book is that American higher education is at a crossroads with regard to student access and equity; to address current challenges, institutions must fundamentally change the ways in which they seek to recruit and retain students; and strategic enrollment management offers a paradigm for bringing together the seemingly disparate goals of student access and institutional financial viability. Achieving these outcomes requires an approach to budgeting different than that employed by most institutions, one that directly links strategic enrollment investments, enrollment projections, and net revenue outcomes to enable more effective campus-wide budgeting and strategic planning. By utilizing the advanced financial planning concepts detailed in this book, institutions can improve their likelihood of increasing net revenue, providing funds to replace those lost through declining federal and state support, and ultimately enhancing affordability and access for all students. An approach to implementing this type of planning is detailed in the following chapters.

Students are at the heart of the higher education enterprise, yet their instruction in the modern university involves a vast infrastructure that simultaneously serves numerous mission-based purposes besides the awarding of degrees.[2] Higher education finances and accounting methods reflect these multiple purposes, some of which are more highly regulated than others, and those financial structures in turn tacitly guide how institutions allocate and invest financial resources to support their multifaceted missions.

The relationship between finance and enrollment extends far beyond students equaling tuition revenue. It is essential that senior leaders understand the full interplay between institutional budgeting and enrollment investments, so that they can develop enrollment plans that not only enroll the requisite numbers of students, but that also provide the financial resources needed to enable institutions to achieve a full range of educational, research, and public service objectives. This chapter provides an overview of institutional finance and the symbiotic relationship between tuition revenues from student enrollments and institutional financial outcomes, and the importance of multifaceted financial analysis as an integral component of effective SEM planning.

---

[2] In addition to instruction, other broad categories of mission-critical programs may include research, health care, and public service. Instructional programs may not even comprise the majority of an institution's financial operations when those include such activities as a hospital, medical clinics or major research enterprise. Non-mission activities of colleges and universities are referred to as "auxiliary enterprises" and typically include campus business activities such as housing, dining, bookstores, and intercollegiate athletics. To some extent management, enterprise data processing, administrative support, and physical plant infrastructure are shared among diverse institutional programs and activities.

CHAPTER THREE
*by* GIL BROWN

# Higher Education Costs and the Role of Tuition

## THE COMPLEX QUESTION OF COLLEGE COSTS

Why does college cost what it does? This is among the issues taken up by the 1998 National Commission on the Cost of Higher Education in "Straight Talk About College Costs and Prices." Precipitated by public pressure over tuition rate increases and "the cost of college," the report begins by describing several alternative interpretations of the term "cost" before settling on a distinction between *cost* as what institutions spend and *price* as what students pay.

A key observation of the Commission was that, unlike the private sector where cost is always less than price, and the difference between the two is profit, the operating costs of higher education are typically higher than the average price paid with the difference between the two being subsidies provided by state appropriations, endowment earnings, private gifts, or other revenues. In contrast to the for-profit equation of "Profit = Price – Cost," the economic structure of higher education is "Cost = Price + Subsidy" (Winston 1997). This means that to the extent that there are subsidies, tuition rates do not reflect full education costs.[3] This model also suggests that two potential routes to moderating higher education costs are to reduce subsidies and/or constrain (tuition) prices, and, in fact, both strategies have been employed by state legislatures in the decade since the publication of this study.

The "Price + Subsidy = Cost" model reveals other stark realities about higher education finances. For one, as prices or subsidies increase, institutions will tend to spend whatever funding is available (*i.e.*, increase costs) for the purpose of advancing their missions. There is seldom a lack of new investments to be made on any campus: annual requests for new or expanded academic and student service programs, additional financial aid, and deferred maintenance and infrastructure enhancements nearly always exceed funds available for such budget additions. A second implication of the cost equation is that given some ongoing level of cost, reductions to subsidies (such as state appropriations) will result in price increases. The more difficult alternatives are to decrease costs or increase the number of paying students; in other words, to increase efficiency. Yet another implication of this cost model is that enrollment increases create a need for some combination of in-

---

[3] Private institutions with significant endowments have long argued that none of their students pay the full costs of their educations, as all benefit from the gift funds supporting the institution. State appropriations function similarly in public institutions, though these institutions typically require that nonresident students do in fact pay their full costs, typically determined by dividing total education and general costs by the total number of students and comparing that "cost per student," including subsidies to the tuition rates paid by nonresident students.

creased subsidies, price increases, or reduced expenditures per student (Winston 2001). Except where excess capacity exists, per student cost reductions can lead to diminished program quality through larger class sizes and overcrowded support services and facilities. The next chapter discusses how SEM can be used to leverage underutilized capacity to increase revenues.

Shortly after the Commission's report was issued, the National Association of College and University Business Officers (NACUBO) developed an instrument designed to identify college costs using a uniform cost accounting methodology that could be applied to any institution. Like the Commission's final report, NACUBO's effort was designed to help educate the public concerning higher education cost drivers. Beginning with audited financial statements, the NACUBO methodology basically subtracted any activities that were not related to students (*e.g.*, sponsored research, auxiliaries, and public service), including overhead costs allocable to those activities, and divided the remaining costs among instruction, student services, institutional and community costs, and financial aid. The methodology calculates an average "cost per undergraduate" and uses a weighting factor applied to that cost to estimate graduate student costs. This instrument has been used by many institutions to assess their uses of funds, but has been proven of limited utility in influencing public policy concerning tuition rates and state appropriation levels.[4]

Unraveling the relationships between higher education costs and revenues is further complicated by the very different timeframes within which budgets, student engagement, and academic culture function. Operating budgets are nearly always annual revenue and expense plans built on available revenue streams; enrollments and tuition revenues impacting budget plans are driven by numerous factors influencing recruitment of new students and retention of current students; and the academic enterprise is built around faculty whose work (and costs) is structured in the context of lifetime tenure. Just as SEM can play a key role in aligning enrollments with underutilized capacity (see Chapter 4), multi-year SEM plans can be

---

[4] An example of the use of this template for all Oregon University System (OUS) institutions can be found at www.ous. edu/state_board/meeting/files/ddoc041105.pdf (p.21 ff.). The NACUBO analysis is designed to separate education costs from other mission and non-mission related costs, and divides education costs into multiple components including instruction, student services, and other categories. The resulting totals describe how education funds are expended, and also serve as a useful comparison to tuition rates charged; in the case of OUS institutions, in-state tuition rates were consistently less than the costs of education, and out-of-state or nonresident tuition rates were higher than actual costs. What this analysis does not directly address is the question posed by legislators, parents, and in this case the OUS Board of *why* higher education costs what it does.

used to align annual budget plans with multi-year revenues and institutional costs (see Chapter 5).

## A BUDGETARY PERSPECTIVE ON HIGHER EDUCATION COSTS

The facilities and grounds of most colleges and universities create a false impression that higher education costs are driven primarily by expenses other than labor. Yet higher education is generally a labor-intensive enterprise, and its cost structure reflects that fact (Bowen 1967). It is not unusual for salary and benefit expenses to make up 90 percent of academic department budgets, and personnel costs typically comprise 70–80 percent of operating budgets for public and private institutions alike.[5] Colleges and universities employ a broad range of support personnel from general office staff to highly specialized laboratory assistants, research administrators, financial managers, and information technology professionals, to name but a few specialties found in a typical college workforce.

The core of the academic enterprise, the faculty, is among the most highly educated individuals within the economy. Research faculty who attract funding support from government and industry are highly marketable as well. As Table 3.1 shows, more highly educated individuals tend to command higher salaries—and higher education as an industry competes in a global labor market for the most talented and highly educated teachers, scholars, and researchers. The competition is with private industry, government and, of course, other higher education institutions.

Most all public colleges and universities publish their annual budgets on the Web in levels of detail varying from institutional summaries to listings of each employee's salary (including faculty); many private institutions publish their annual financial statements on the Web as well. The percentage of total costs devoted to instruction

---

[5] These ratios vary significantly at different institutions; deductions such as depreciation expense and interest on debt service can significantly reduce this ratio in institutional financial statements. The author bases these ratios on experiences at diverse public and private research universities. At George Mason University, a regional public institution with enrollments of approximately thirty thousand students, for the 2008–2009 fiscal year 79 percent of education and general operating costs are budgeted for salaries (62%) and related benefits (17%). Operating budget funds are those most significantly impacted by revenue streams such as tuition and state appropriations. An issue paper titled "Frequently Asked Questions About College Costs" released at the request of Charles Miller, Chairman of The Secretary of Education's Commission on the Future of Higher Education begins with these phrases: "1. Why does college cost so much? Colleges are labor-intensive. a. On average, 75 percent of the costs to run a college are related to personnel expenses, including benefits." Retrieved August 4, 2008 from www.ed.gov/about/bdscomm/list/hiedfuture/reports/dickeson2.pdf.

## Table 3.1

**AVERAGE INCOME BY EDUCATIONAL
ATTAINMENT OF HOUSEHOLDER, 2006**

| Educational Attainment | Mean | |
|---|---|---|
| | $ | %[1] |
| Total, 25 yrs & over | 79,073 | 100 |
| Less than 9th grade | 36,323 | 46 |
| 9th to 12th grade, no diploma | 40,185 | 51 |
| High school graduate (includes equivalency) | 59,548 | 75 |
| Some college, no degree | 71,147 | 90 |
| Associate degree | 76,673 | 97 |
| Bachelor's degree or more | 120,685 | 153 |
| Bachelor's degree | 110,072 | 139 |
| Master's degree | 128,461 | 162 |
| Professional degree | 168,880 | 214 |
| Doctorate degree | 159,719 | 202 |

[1] Percentage of total mean

**SOURCE:** U.S. Census Bureau, Current Population Survey, 2007 Annual Social and Economic Supplement.

varies significantly among institutions.[6] There is, of course, a multi-tiered structure to instructional costs. At many institutions, graduate teaching assistants—PhDs in training—also teach courses for which they are paid a fraction of faculty salaries and typically receive tuition waivers. Part-time adjunct faculty members are typically paid "by the course" at rates far below the equivalent cost for a full-time faculty member and are increasingly relied upon to provide instruction. Increased reliance on graduate assistants and adjunct faculty to provide instruction arguably diminishes the quality of the classroom experience, and insulates undergraduates from the benefits of collateral research efforts of faculty in research institutions.[7]

Beyond personnel costs, colleges and universities face a mix of expenses similar to those of private industry: a long list of regulatory compliance costs, rising energy prices, litigation and risk management costs, and overall inflation on goods and services. For many institutions, the costs of information technology involve not only equipping students and faculty with the most current networking, software, and computer technologies, but also with access to online library resources including

---

[6] Audited financial statements for both public and private institutions will separately show annual expenditures for instruction in addition to other categories. Academic support, plant operation and maintenance, institutional support, public service, student service, and research are the other categories.

[7] See discussion in Dill 2003.

specialized databases, periodicals, and instructional resources. Ongoing improvements in instrumentation and computer simulation technologies require continuous investments to maintain research laboratories. Facilities are typically funded by private gifts, public appropriations, or bonds paid over terms of twenty or more years. Finally, there is the increasing cost of institutional financial aid in the forms of scholarships and tuition discounts.

From the budgetary perspective most institutions have been growing in numbers of students, instructional expenditures per student, and research expenditures over the last decade, while from the revenue perspective, state government support for instruction and federal government support for research has not kept pace with increased levels of institutional spending. Tuition and other revenue sources have been left to pick up the slack (Hossler 2004).

The mathematics of these equations is simple; the accounting that drives those equations, described later in this chapter, is not so simple. Table 3.2 illustrates annual revenue and expense changes for a hypothetical state-supported institution with a $100 million operating budget (80 percent of which is for labor expenses). This hypothetical institution receives 60 percent of its funding from state support, which is increasing by 1 percent, while providing 4 percent salary increases and no inflationary increases for other expenses.

This example reveals a funding dynamic that has accompanied declining ratios of state support—how tuition can increase at over twice the rate of overall budget growth, based solely on the rate of salary increases exceeding the rate of non-tuition revenue growth funding increases. The same dynamic that exists for state support can be applied to other revenue sources (*e.g.*, research or gift funding) for which tuition revenues may be called upon to meet base operating expenses.

While simplified, Table 3.2 also illustrates some very common dynamics of annual higher education budgets. The only net expense increases are to salary costs (usually these include benefit costs as well), and in order to hold "all other" costs (including utilities, supplies, etc.) at the "base" level, the institution must realize efficiencies or reduce expenses in some categories to offset inflation in other categories. From the institutional standpoint this would be a frugal budget—3.2 percent increases are not excessive—driven by the modest increase in state support. To achieve this expense growth outcome, however, the level of "tuition support" must increase by over twice the rate of expense increases. If enrollments do not

## Table 3.2

### AN ILLUSTRATION OF ANNUAL CHANGES IN REVENUE AND EXPENSE COMPONENTS

|  | Base | Increase | Total | % Change |
|---|---|---|---|---|
| **Revenues** | | | | |
| State support | 60,000,000 | 600,000 | 60,600,000 | 1.0 |
| Tuition support | 40,000,000 | 2,600,000 | 42,600,000 | 6.5 |
| Total budget | 100,000,000 | 3,200,000 | 103,200,000 | 3.2 |
| **Expenses** | | | | |
| Salary costs | 80,000,000 | 3,200,000 | 83,200,000 | 4.0 |
| All other | 20,000,000 | 0 | 20,000,000 | 0.0 |
| Total budget | 100,000,000 | 3,200,000 | 103,200,000 | 3.2 |

change, this would require a 6.5 percent increase in tuition to realize a 3.2 percent expense budget increase. If increased enrollments *do* contribute to increased tuition support—for example, rate increases account for 5 percent and enrollments for 1.5 percent of the increase in tuition support—even further efficiencies would be required on the expense side in order to serve more students.

The "Delaware Study," a comprehensive discipline-specific analysis of longitudinal cost data collected from numerous institutions, claims that "(t)here is no pure cause and effect relationship between price (tuition) and cost (what institutions actually expend...)" (Middaugh 2005, p.8). Tuition and fees are intended to cover instruction and instruction-related costs. However, the *funding sources* for instructional faculty, classrooms, and related costs are not tied to tuition and fees alone but may include subsidies from endowment earnings or state appropriations. If "Cost = Price + Subsidy," then "Price = Cost – Subsidy"; while the value students receive in the form of instructional expenditures on their behalf should be less than the price they pay, the extent to which their payments cover costs varies with the levels of subsidy.

In other words, decreasing levels of subsidies whether in the form of governmental appropriations, private gifts, or endowment earnings result in students having to pay a higher proportion of the total costs of their educations. At the institutional level, funding sources such as tuition are called upon to fill any and all gaps that exist in more restricted areas of revenue activity. Thus, when examining institutional costs in the context of complex missions serving numerous constituencies, tuition is revealed as the single most significant revenue lever institutions have at their disposal to fulfill these missions.

## HIGHER EDUCATION BUDGETING AND ACCOUNTING

Budget planning in higher education varies significantly from institution to institution based on state requirements and institutional history, yet there are four general phases to which most budget cycles adhere on an annual basis (Brown 2005):

- Stage 1—Budget development ("the budget process")
- Stage 2—Implementation ("booking the budget")
- Stage 3—Monitoring (budget management)
- Stage 4—Evaluation (variance analysis)

Unless budget crises develop in the course of the fiscal year, interest in the budget cycle generally peaks during Stage 1, declines in Stages 2 and 3, and recaptures attention in Stage 4 in the context of the subsequent budget cycle (Brown). It is in the course of budget development (Stage 1) that most attention is focused on addressing institutional priorities.

A complex university budget may contain tens of thousands of summary budget lines. The starting point—or "base"—for higher education budgets includes the physical infrastructure of libraries, classrooms, laboratories, offices, and other facilities used by students, instructional and research faculty, and support personnel. On the expense side, salaries and benefit costs for faculty and support staff combined with plant operation and maintenance typically make up the bulk of the budget, and addressing cost inflation in these expenses alone requires significant new resources each year. As engines of change, however, for universities to merely "do the same thing" as last year is seldom doing enough. Programs evolve and expand in response to legislative mandates, constituent needs, and market opportunities, and more often than not these initiatives require some level of institutional financial support that cannot be redirected from other activities without curtailing those programs which also serve some constituency or mission-critical need.

Rules governing higher education accounting and financial reporting are shaped by the multiplicity of public and private constituencies these institutions serve. Students pay for courses; corporations pay for training and research; government agencies pay to support activities ranging from graduate student training and laboratory science to highly specialized research facilities; and patients and their insurers pay for health care; the list goes on and on. Non-profit organizations, including colleges and universities, hold funds received in "trust" to serve these numerous purposes;

financial reporting mechanisms are designed to show stewardship of and account for the uses of funds to benefit these multiple constituencies. It is fair to say that these constituencies expect—and in some cases demand—that the financial investments they make in the services provided will approximate the costs of providing those services.

To facilitate clear financial reporting in this complex setting, the "fund accounting" approach used by higher education institutions is designed to track revenues by source and expenses by program. Sources include tuition and fees, government appropriations, private gifts, grants and contracts, endowment income, educational sales and services, health care services, auxiliary enterprises, and other sources. These revenue streams are in turn tied to specific programmatic and support functions including instruction, research, public service, academic support, student services, institutional support, plant operation and maintenance, auxiliary enterprises, and scholarships and fellowships. Fund accounting establishes walls of separation to ensure that funds received to fulfill specific purposes can only be used for those purposes (Brown 2005).

Both revenues and expenses tied to various program activities are separately tracked according to their sources, and restrictions placed on their use. Unrestricted funds generally include tuition and fees charged for services, recovery of indirect costs from sponsored research, and gifts given to the institution without any strings (restrictions) attached. Unrestricted funds can be used for any purpose consistent with the institution's mission including instruction, academic support, research, public service, institutional support, or plant operation and maintenance. Restricted funds include direct costs of sponsored research and gifts intended by their donors to support specific uses such as capital projects, programs, or services. State funds are similarly appropriated to provide either general program support or targeted purposes.

Complexities arise when the same individuals and facilities are funded from multiple revenue sources to perform multiple program activities. It is not unusual for a single faculty member to teach a class in the morning (instruction), give an off-campus lecture for lunch (public service), serve on an institutional committee in the afternoon (institutional support), and spend the remainder of the day doing scholarly or laboratory research (research). If the research involves a paid graduate research assistant whose assistantship position is tied to enrollment in a graduate program, the faculty member may be simultaneously performing both instruction and research.

Most striking about institutional budget processes is all the funds that are *not* included in budget allocations, and the extent to which "new" revenues are consumed by maintaining current programs, responding to new regulatory requirements, and addressing plant operation and maintenance costs. For the most part, restricted funds are not available for allocation; sponsor or donor restrictions determine how and for what purposes those funds can be utilized. Auxiliary enterprises function as stand-alone nonprofit operations within the institution; room and board revenues do not provide support for instruction or other mission-critical activities. In a large institution these funds may account for hundreds of millions of dollars that are not part of the base operating budget equation.

## TUITION REVENUE AND RESEARCH SUPPORT

There is some degree of flexibility within fund accounting, and the greatest flexibility is in the form of current unrestricted revenues such as tuition that can be used to fund any mission-related purpose. Sponsored program ("research") activity provides an example of some of the characteristics and limitations of fund accounting that can create added pressures on tuition revenue.[8]

Sponsored research typically involves funds that can only be used for restricted purposes related to the sponsored project and, for most federal research grants, facilities and administrative ("indirect") cost reimbursements. Project budgets to perform the research are developed by principle investigators (PIs) and approved by the sponsor (often a federal agency). These budgets may include salaries for the PI and others such as graduate research assistants, as well as the cost of equipment. Often project budgets are negotiated so the university contributes ("cost shares") a portion of the total project cost. Funds provided by the sponsor to the institution for project costs are restricted funds and can only be used for the specific research project costs. When research funds cover a portion of a faculty member's salary, this "frees" budget funds that otherwise would have paid some portion of the faculty salary for the period of the project. In addition to these funds, the sponsor may

---

[8] While the question of cross-subsidization of research by instructional revenues among research institutions is widely debated (see Dill 2003), the debate hinges not on the question of whether instructional revenues are used to support research—they are—but of the value of research activities one assigns to the instructional enterprise, and whether that benefit justifies the levels of instructional revenue contributions that do in fact occur.

provide unrestricted indirect cost reimbursements for the project based on a negotiated indirect cost rate.

Indirect cost reimbursement rates are negotiated every few years based on an
analysis of past research activity and past institutional costs either completely or
partially supporting the research enterprise. In this process institutions and the federal government agree on a "base year" upon which to assess institutional indirect
costs, and an analysis of that year's activity results in a rate that serves as the starting point for subsequent negotiation. In the negotiation process, institutions may
argue to include additional costs (*e.g.*, for new research facilities not reflected in the
base year) and the government may "disallow" certain costs associated with activities other than research. The process for calculating indirect cost rates is complex
and includes a "cap" of 26 percent on administrative costs, but the decisive formula
is a relatively simple division equation with total research costs as the denominator
and facilities and administrative costs as the numerator.[9]

Within institutions, indirect cost revenues from research can be used for any
purpose—they are unrestricted funds—consistent with the original unrestricted
source of the expenditures these revenues are intended to reimburse. Yet it is common for institutions to "reinvest" at least some portion of these funds to promote
the research program, since the research program is responsible for generating the
revenues. If, in turn, the funds are used to support so-called departmental or institutionally funded research, adding to the research cost numerator, the long term
impact on indirect cost reimbursement will be a decrease in the rate and reduced future cost recovery. Similarly, when institutions "cost share" (do not recover the full
indirect cost rate) research projects, the effect on future calculations is a decrease in
rates and recovery. The conclusion of these complex calculations is that research activities require some degree of subsidy from other funding sources such as tuition.

Faculty researchers generally perceive indirect costs as paying for overhead (facilities and administration) for which they do not receive benefits equal to the indirect cost charges involved. There is not a grant-by-grant correspondence between
indirect costs charged to the grant and facilities or administrative support provided
for a specific grant. Rather, much like instructional costs, the total cost of indi-

---

[9] Office of Management and Budget Circular A-21, "Cost Principles for Educational Institutions" prescribes the process
for determining allowable indirect costs including the 26 percent cap. Indirect costs are intended to be costs
incurred by institutions in support of the research enterprise and so are added on to direct costs – salaries and
equipment for example – to actually perform the research work.

rect grant support is averaged over all grants. A plea comparable to that of the PI claiming excessive indirect cost charges would be a student tallying instructor salaries for a given term and concluding that the tuition being charged was more than was needed to pay the faculty and overhead charges associated with the student's specific needs for that term. Tuition is similarly "averaged" over numerous courses, faculty, facility, and support requirements.

These transactions all play out in great detail within fund accounting systems. Accounting wants to be precise and explicit, and it is essential that institutions get their accounting "right." Many funding scandals of the past two decades could largely be traced to improper accounting for revenues or expenses.[10] A transaction miscoding here or there can make it appear that monies intended for one purpose were used for another. The results can be embarrassing and expensive.[11] Accountants are thus understandably careful and cautious in their treatment of financial information and transaction processing. Reports of past financial activity (accounting) must be accurate and complete within prescribed definitions and recording practices.

It is the unrestricted revenue stream that is left to cover expenditures that are not allowable on grants or other restricted funds. For example, administrative costs attributable to research but in excess of the 26 percent cap must be borne by unrestricted sources. In other fund groups there are similar complexities involved. For example "auxiliary enterprises" are activities that support but do not constitute mission-critical programs. These include room and board, intercollegiate athletics, the bookstore, and other campus retail services. Public service, including hospital, physician, and veterinary services involve similar complexities. These various transactions may be regulated by different accounting rules spelled out in state and federal regulations.

---

[10] Federally funded research is among the most restrictive revenue sources for colleges and universities, involving "time and effort" reporting systems, lists of unallowable expenditures (*i.e.*, expenses that cannot be charged to grants), indirect cost calculations, and cost accounting standards that are sufficiently complex that there is literally an industry of high level accountants who make their careers in this specific practice area. The typical research faculty member who knows and cares little about accounting or "paperwork" can place institutions at great financial risk by ignoring these accounting rules in the routine course of business.

[11] The most notorious example of accounting errors leading to embarrassing (and largely uninformed) public reports is the case of Stanford University in the early 1990s. The final resolution explaining some of the issues can be found at http://news-service.stanford.edu/pr/94/941018Arc4090.html.

## SUMMARY

For most colleges and universities tuition remains the most significant and controllable source of revenues that can be used to support numerous components of complex missions. However, public sentiment against soaring tuition rates and resulting legislative caps on tuition increasingly threaten its controllability by state-governed institutions. In both public and private research universities tuition revenues contribute to stimulating research efforts that carry into the classroom and are unlikely to be funded by other sources (Dill 2003). For both public and private institutions, tuition revenues play an increasingly pivotal role in supporting mission-critical activities beyond instruction.

As tuition becomes ever more important, accurate enrollment projections take on further financial significance. Revenues can only be applied to planned expenditures if the revenues are accurately projected and incorporated into the budget plan. With increasing reliance on tuition revenues, the modeling described in Chapter 5 is a critical component to institutions responding effectively to balancing their budgets in the face of shifting subsidies, whether those subsidies are from endowments or state appropriations. Heavily endowed institutions typically use multi-year averaging of investment gains to guide endowment spending plans. State institutions watch the legislative process unfold, year to year or biennium to biennium, and prepare numerous contingency plans as state appropriation levels are finalized. In both cases, the context within which linking SEM and financial planning can shape a paradigm for increasing access and realizing other nonfinancial institutional goals and objectives is one within which tuition revenue already plays a key role in funding the academic enterprise.

CHAPTER FOUR
*by* GIL BROWN

# A SEM Perspective on Budgeting

As described in the preceding chapter, tuition revenue plays a key role in balancing the higher education cost equation not only for instruction-related costs but for other mission-critical activities as well. As the importance of tuition revenue increases, so does the importance of understanding the complex dynamics of how enrollment goals intersect with pricing and discounting decisions in order to achieve both financial and nonfinancial campus goals.[12] A failure to understand this complex web of factors can result in enrollment problems that undermine financial stability and institutional goal attainment.

This chapter examines why SEM is key to institutions in realizing both operational efficiencies and sufficient revenues to fund their operations, while fulfilling their public missions and the promise of access to higher education. Understanding how tuition revenues from enrollments flow into institutions over a predictable time horizon makes possible financial planning for a broad range of institutional outcomes, including increased access to instructional programs via the provision of institutional need-based financial aid. A process and model for achieving these outcomes is presented in Chapter 5.

## PUBLIC GOOD, PRIVATE BENEFITS AND ACCESS

Institutional diversity is frequently identified as one of the fundamental strengths of American higher education. Institutional mission statements may alternately emphasize the creation of new knowledge through scholarship and research, the training of students in a specific profession, advancement of arts and letters through undergraduate education, economic and workforce development, or service to a particular community or geographic region. However else they may differ—public or private, with open enrollment or rigorous admission standards, focused largely on instruction or research—what the missions of all non-proprietary colleges and universities have in common is the service of some public good.[13] At the same time,

---

[12] Broadly these dynamics can be described as the inherent tension between the competing goals of access, affordability, and quality (see Heller, 2001, for a discussion of access, affordability and accountability).

[13] From the granting of Harvard College's tax-exempt charter in 1650 "that may conduce to the education of the English and Indian youth of this country, in knowledge and godliness" (Harvard Charter of 1650) through the 1787 Northwest Ordinance's declaration that "[r]eligion, morality, and knowledge, being necessary to good government and the happiness of mankind, schools and the means of education shall forever be encouraged," and passage of the 1862 Morrill Act establishing land grant institutions in each of the United States, service to some public good has been a defining characteristic of American higher education.

students and other recipients of higher education services derive private benefit from those services.

The dual public and private benefits served by institutions is reflected in the combination of public and private financial sources that fund them. As discussed in Chapter 2, tuition-dependent private institutions have long used tuition pricing and "discounting" strategies to balance revenue attainment and enrollment goals, in effect charging differential tuition rates depending on a variety of factors including the ability to pay. Public research universities typically combine several components of mission, with some levels of access promised to state residents who may benefit from their many services. As tuition dependence for public institutions increase in response to the state support reductions described in Chapter 1, these institutions as well are looking to discounting strategies to achieve similar ends.[14]

The ability to attend college regardless of one's ability to pay—access—is a defining characteristic of public institutions, with the benefits accrued by individual students simultaneously serving important societal needs (Brittan 2003). For these institutions in particular, changing funding landscapes have brought issues of access and affordability head-to-head with existential challenges concerning the public and private purposes these institutions simultaneously serve (Zemsky 2003).

## USING SEM TO INCREASE PROGRAM QUALITY AND EXPAND ACCESS

The analytical toolkit that has evolved through the practice of SEM offers a solution to the issue of financing complex missions and infrastructure while balancing competing commitments to student access, program quality, and affordability. Consistent with those missions, the use of SEM in public institutions arguably must avoid the pitfalls of diminished access that some have argued discount practices foster (Davis 2003).

A concise demand curve describing the relationship between tuition rates, enrollments, and discounts is put forth by David Breneman in "Liberal Arts Colleges: Thriving, Surviving or Endangered?" Tuition discounting can be used as a strategy to maximize net revenues from those able and willing to pay tuition at a given rate while reducing the effective rate for those unable or unwilling to pay at higher rates

---

[14] "Not only are significant amounts of institutional aid in the public sector being distributed based on criteria other than need, but a high proportion of dollars are allocated to students whose financial circumstances would permit them to enroll without these subsidies" (Baum 2006, p. 9).

(Breneman 1994). Discounts are applied to encourage enrollment by students that the institution wishes to attract but who may not be willing or able to pay tuition at higher rates. At the same time, students both willing and able to pay tuition at higher rates are not offered discounts. The extent to which higher sticker prices attract or discourage applications and subsequent enrollments and predicting whether a given student will or will not attend based on the discount provided are among the variables institutional pricing and discounting strategies must consider.

Much criticism of tuition discounting rests on the application of discounts to students who could (and might) otherwise pay higher tuition rates, in other words for merit-based purposes, rather than to expand access to those unable to pay.[15] This is not a function of discounting per se, but of *a particular application* of discounting strategies to ends other than maximization of net revenues. The analytical tools of SEM are indifferent to the purposes they serve. Tuition discounting is one such tool that can serve many masters—increasing access among them. For example, discounting rates for students unable to pay the full rate, by definition, increases access for those students.

For the private institutions Breneman examines, a combination of optimum enrollments and net revenue attainment is the goal of discounting strategies; in other words discounting is not purely a net revenue maximizing strategy as many of the institutions could meet their enrollment goals with full-paying students and thus realize higher net revenue, yet opt for less net revenue and the more diverse student body afforded by their discounting strategies. Setting too low a price for all students may ensure ample enrollments and attainment of all nonfinancial objectives but generate insufficient revenue to pay for a high quality instructional program. In setting institutional pricing and discounting rates nonfinancial factors are balanced with realizing the levels of net revenue necessary to actually operate the institution in setting institutional pricing and discounting rates.

Full-pay tuition rates receive significant public and legislative attention and for public institutions require a sound public policy basis. Setting the full-pay tuition

---

[15] Both Davis in "Unintended Consequences of Tuition Discounting" (Lumina Foundation, 2003) and Baum in "Tuition Discounting: Not Just a Private College Practice" (The College Board, 2006) find evidence that public institutions utilize discounts in this manner. Consistent with Winston's cost formulation cited in Chapter 3, public institutions faced with increased tuition dependency can financially benefit more from *unsubsidized* nonresident enrollments than from increasing resident enrollments. Is this counter to their public missions? The institutions would argue not: nonresident tuition revenues are filling a revenue gap resulting from reduced state appropriations, and net revenues realized from nonresident discounting strategies are maintaining program *quality* for all students.

price is a significant strategic decision that, if not mandated by legislative fiat, can be based on the history of full-pay student enrollments and a gauging of competitive price inflation, in other words based on the price elasticity for a given institution. For public institutions, applying discounts based on financial need can ensure access to those unable to pay, while higher tuition rates for those both willing and able to pay can maximize net revenues available to fund the institutional mission. This strategy is essentially an extension of the differential tax burdens placed on state residents who would otherwise be paying increased taxes based on their ability to pay in order to fund increased state appropriations to support the institution. For those unable to pay, some revenue baseline of external financial aid accrues to the institution (*e.g.*, Pell Grants). For those able to pay, the decision whether to attend an institution or not—willingness to pay—depends on perceptions of program quality and pricing considerations.

A reasonable starting point for public institutions is to model the full-pay rate at the average cost of instruction plus the average discount less state support per student. This formula may yield a result that is outside the bounds of an institution's price elasticity if, for example, a disproportionately high percentage of its students are unable to afford to pay instructional costs (resulting in a high discount rate). This formula is unashamedly designed to transfer costs from those unable to pay to those both willing and able to pay and is in that sense a transfer of wealth strategy not unlike the differential tax burdens it replaces. In the event there is inadequate wealth to transfer—students who are able to pay are not willing to pay the resulting costs—identifying nonresident students both willing and able to pay rates that fully fund instructional costs (as required by most states) becomes an essential strategy for institutional financial equilibrium with discounting strategies applied to maximize net revenues.

Yet there are significant dangers attendant to this strategy: institutions can price themselves out of consideration by students who "self-select" not to apply for admission, not realizing the sticker price may be more than they will be asked to pay, and discounts may inadvertently be provided to students who would be willing and able to pay more than is asked, resulting in a loss of net revenue to the institution. Both are significant issues for public institutions considering using this SEM strategy. Both outreach programs designed to encourage the pursuit of higher education and rigorous analysis of historic enrollment data are components of effective institutional responses to these pitfalls of discounting (Breneman 1994).

Keep in mind from the foregoing discussion that at most public institutions, resident students do not pay the full costs of their educations even at the "sticker price" (before discounting tuition). It can be argued that higher income residents attending state institutions have borne a higher tax burden to provide state funding, and so increasing public institution tuition places an even greater burden on families who have already contributed more than their fair share to education costs. Need-based discounting for residents is, in effect, an extension of differential tax burdens based on income level.

As outlined above, the public policies have a common end goal: ensuring access to high quality programs and services. In the case of tax burdens, the state imposes a funding requirement on its citizenry in recognition of the public good served by higher education institutions. In the case of using SEM to increase access, a combination of economic incentives and consumer choices can be used to drive the same public policy outcomes.

## BUDGETING ENROLLMENT OUTCOMES

Higher education efficiency requires, first and foremost, that investments already being made are leveraged to their greatest advantage without sacrificing quality, and here SEM plays a significant role in aligning enrollments with capacity. A second element in the efficiency equation that aligns SEM with financial, individual student, and public policy goals is to increase retention and graduation rates. Finally, SEM modeling at the levels of precision set forth in the model in Chapter 5 provides long-term revenue outlooks that facilitate greatly improved multi-year institutional financial planning and thus provides a sound foundation for enhanced access funded by tuition revenues.

As tuition becomes increasingly important to funding ongoing operations of public institutions, and as discounting strategies designed to meet institutional goals beyond net revenue generation are integrated into SEM plans, accurate enrollment projections for specific enrollment funnels (or market segments) take on increasing financial significance. Revenues can only be applied to planned expenditures if the revenues are accurately planned for and incorporated into the budget plan. When significant net revenue differentials exist within specific categories of students (*e.g.*, resident undergraduates), greater enrollment forecasting precision is needed to optimize institutional financial planning. Finally, the alignment of enrollments with capacity has significant institutional cost implications.

For the budget development process, a multi-year plan affords several significant advantages that have lead to this model's adoption by many institutions. Seed funding can be phased and tracked over multiple fiscal periods, and funding priorities can be established outside the constraints of annual revenues. Multi-year modeling is also particularly well-suited to planning tuition revenues. As enrollment managers know well, recruitment results in any given year have multi-year consequences for their institutions. One year's enrollment outcomes can have significant long-term consequences for both institutional revenues and expenses.

Again some very basic arithmetic demonstrates the financial significance of enrollment activities. Table 4.1 outlines the multi-year financial implications of a one-year enrollment variance of twenty students assuming an initial tuition rate of $7,500 with 5 percent per year tuition increases and 80 percent annual retention year to year.

## Table 4.1

MODEL OF TUITION REVENUES FROM 20
STUDENT ENROLLMENT VARIANCE

|        | Tuition Rate | n  | Revenues |
|--------|--------------|----|----------|
| Year 1 | 7,500        | 20 | 150,000  |
| Year 2 | 7,875        | 16 | 126,000  |
| Year 3 | 8,269        | 13 | 107,497  |
| Year 4 | 8,682        | 10 | 86,820   |

Given these assumptions, over a four-year period tuition revenues of roughly $470,000 are at stake. If these students can be accommodated by existing course sections, instructors, and student services, this twenty student variance results in no marginal cost increases and so these revenues are available for allocation to meet virtually any mission-related institutional priority. As a budget variance in the first year—unexpected revenue, consequently unplanned for on the expense side as well—the $150,000 in Year 1 revenues may end up covering shortfalls in other revenue categories, over-expenditures compared to budget, or unfunded institutional priorities identified midyear or remaining from the previous budget planning cycle.

Given annual budget planning cycles and the importance of meeting revenue goals—after all, the bulk of those funds are supporting salaries—"windfall" revenues of the sort described above resulting from conservative enrollment projections are not uncommon. Budget administrators are reluctant to risk committing financial resources that may not materialize, and enrollment managers are similarly hesitant to risk taking the blame for midyear budget reductions should enrollments not materialize. Sound budgeting practice balances risk with risk aversion by forecasting the most likely outcomes and stipulating contingency plans within reasonable error rates for the forecast. Applying such a budgetary strategy to enrollment (and tuition) projections eases some of the pressure on enrollment managers to avoid over-projecting at all costs. In the context of Table 4.1, a contingency budget plan may have stipulated that the $150,000 in Year 1 excess revenues would be used to provide additional program support to a specific area. For the subsequent years (two to four, and perhaps beyond four years) the known variance from Year 1 projected enrollments should be incorporated into enrollment and tuition projections, and consequently those revenues would be available for allocation in the normal budget process.

Table 4.2 takes these assumptions one step further and posits that the "one-time variance" can be repeated over multiple fiscal years:

With no change in tuition rate or retention assumptions, by Year 4 the addition of twenty additional incoming students each year has produced additional revenues of over $500,000 and increased enrollment by fifty-nine students. From an institutional budget planning perspective the one-time allocation of $150,000 in response to a revenue windfall is significantly different from a predictable future revenue stream that may or may not entail increased costs. The $500,000 in additional operating revenue generated by these enrollments in Year 4 is the equivalent of a $10 million endowment gift.[16] Over the four years covered in Table 4.2, it adds over $1.35 million in revenues that can be applied to expense requirements.

## Table 4.2

### MULTI-YEAR EXTENSION OF A 20 STUDENT ANNUAL ENROLLMENT VARIANCE

| Year | Tuition Rate | Cohorts | | | | Revenues |
|------|------|------|------|------|------|------|
| | | 1 | 2 | 3 | 4 | |
| 1 | 7,500 | 20 | | | | 150,000 |
| 2 | 7,875 | 16 | 20 | | | 283,500 |
| 3 | 8,269 | 13 | 16 | 20 | | 405,181 |
| 4 | 8,682 | 10 | 13 | 16 | 20 | 512,238 |

---

[16] The metric of endowment equivalence is frequently used to emphasize the significance of cost reduction or revenue enhancement efforts. Assuming a 5 percent annual payout, a $10 million endowment gift would contribute $500,000 to the operating budget. On most campuses the potential uses of a $10 million endowment gift may consume significant time and management attention; the implication is that activity with the comparable annual financial impact deserves comparable attention. Given the multi-year implications of much enrollment management activity, as this

Both budget and SEM practitioners understand that variances of the sort presented in the figures above are by no means unusual. What tends to be unusual in practice is the discrete, multi-year treatment of new unplanned activity such as is represented in these figures. Base revenue and expense budgets would be adjusted, and institutional planning would continue in its normal fashion. What these figures demonstrate, however, is the *significant financial impact of relatively modest changes in enrollments*. In Tables 4.1 (on page 54) and 4.2 (on page 55) the additional enrollments are presented as "variances" to plan. What if these increases were discretely planned and use of the revenues allocated to achieve nonfinancial enrollment goals such as increasing access?

Budget planning when using significant institutional funds for need-based financial aid requires increased accuracy, not only in projecting the numbers of students who will be enrolling, but also in the levels of tuition those students who do enroll will be paying. In effect, some portion of revenues from students paying higher than the average "net price" for tuition supports those students paying less than the average. The budget and enrollment plans must reflect such levels of specificity as the average net price to be paid, and enrollments must be managed to those targets; within that context, it is entirely possible to plan for enrollments that reflect lower net prices (increased discount) based on financial need. It was asserted earlier in this chapter that SEM tools can be used to realize such outcomes, *i.e.*, to simultaneously address the balance between access, quality, and affordability. Absent revenue additions from other sources such as external grants, appropriations or gift funds, or cost containment, it is possible that SEM strategies combined with careful budget planning may offer the *only* way to achieve a balance between these competing priorities.

Finally, the alignment of enrollments with capacity is another way SEM strategies can promote the efficient use of institutional resources while at the same time expanding access and affordability. Underenrolled programs and courses provide opportunities for institutions to realize additional revenues without incurring marginal cost increases.

Critical as they are, making accurate projections alone is not enough to address the funding needs of public institutions in an era of declining state support. Consistent with their missions, such institutions must simultaneously maximize access

---

example shows, variances in activity can quickly reach the threshold of significance when expressed as endowment equivalence.

to their programs and the quality of the programs provided to their constituents. Access is a function of the opportunity to attend—is there room in the program, and is it affordable?—and quality is a function of adequate material and human resources available to offer programs or, in a word, money. Like the private institutions that gave rise to SEM practices described in Chapter 2, public institutions today face the challenge of increasing net revenues to support their programs with the added complexity of maintaining or increasing access to those programs.

## SUMMARY

The increased reliance on tuition revenues by public colleges and universities necessitates greater coordination of budget and enrollment planning activities; private institutions long accustomed to depending on tuition revenues can also benefit from the integration of multi-year enrollment and budget plans. While budgeting and enrollment planning has historically emphasized annual goal-setting and evaluation, placing both planning processes on a multi-year horizon improves the quality of information available to make revenue allocation and program investment decisions. Beyond this, accurate enrollment revenue projections can be combined with targeted strategies to achieve both financial and nonfinancial institutional goals.

CHAPTER FIVE
*by* BOB BONTRAGER
*and* GIL BROWN

# Integrating Enrollment and Budget Planning

## The SEM Planning Model

The interplay, and common conflicts, between institutional and student interests may be most stark in the context of financial issues—most specifically, the quest to keep higher education as affordable as possible for the largest number of students while maintaining viable, sustainable financial outcomes for the institution. The connection between enrollment projections and budget outcomes has always been evident at private institutions, with their history of tuition-driven budgets. Public institutions have become increasingly tuition-driven as well, given the decline in state support discussed in earlier chapters.

While the connection between enrollment and budget outcomes is commonly recognized, it is often at a basic level that fails to capture the dynamic interplay of enrollment and institutional finance. This chapter will describe the state of enrollment projecting and related institutional budgeting practices, and the limitations of that approach. An alternative model, the SEM Planning Model, will be described, along with examples of how the model may be used to facilitate enrollment and budget planning at the institutional and individual initiative levels. Implementing this type of model represents a sea change in the way most institutions operate. As such it offers an opportunity to address the kind of fundamental change called for by many in the higher education community, as referenced in earlier chapters.

## CURRENT PRACTICES

Many institutions develop their enrollment and budget projections based on a simple planning model:

- Project budget numbers for the next one or two years based on prior budget allocations to institutional units and consider anticipated changes in key inputs (for example, mandated budget cuts, increased health care costs, new or eliminated programs).
- Observe the resulting bottom line budget outcome, which is usually not as favorable as desired.
- Determine the number of students required to increase revenue and achieve a more desirable bottom line budget outcome. This becomes the enrollment projection.

The limitations of this basic approach include the following:

- It places the institution in a short-term planning mindset that primarily looks backward to prior performance, rather than forward to a desired future.

- It artificially truncates the enrollment planning process, including required investments related to recruitment and retention strategies, and fails to account for the longer time frame required for specific strategies to take hold and achieve the desired results.

- It fails to account for the range of investments and costs associated with recruiting and retaining different types of students; this leaves open the very real possibility that the enrollment goals may be met, but the costs associated with recruiting and retaining the additional students will be greater than the added revenue the students bring to the institution.

- It relegates enrollment and enrollment managers to secondary status in the strategic budgeting and planning process, contrary to the actual role of enrollment as the largest annual source of revenue for most campuses.

- It focuses on enrollment as a number, often as a single aggregate number, rather than on the concept of enrollment as a reflection of institutional mission. As a result, institutions can too easily lose sight of desired outcomes that are other than budgetary, including goals for access, equity, and student success.

## THE SEM PLANNING MODEL

While the factors listed above describe many institutions, others will find themselves at various stages of more effective planning. Regardless of an institution's current planning status, most can improve the *strategic* dimension their planning efforts by applying the more advanced concepts of strategic enrollment management.

The SEM Planning Model is a rubric for bringing together enrollment and financial planning to facilitate more effective strategic planning for colleges and universities, enabling them to achieve not only their desired budget outcomes, but also to fulfill their broader mission-driven goals. The model brings together development of comprehensive enrollment goals, strategic enrollment investments, measurable enrollment outcomes, net revenue results, institutional budget outcomes, and strategic reinvestment strategies. By tracking these factors over an extended, ten-year planning horizon, institutions can create decision packages that facilitate strategic planning at the institutional and unit level, including both administrative and academic functions. Implementation of the SEM Planning Model occurs in phases.

## Phase 1:
## Developing Comprehensive Enrollment Goals

Many institutions operate on the simple premise that they want more students than they have now. Those institutions would have difficulty stating how many students would be "enough" or what student profile would best fulfill the institution's mission. Determining an institution's optimum enrollment profile is an extraordinarily complex undertaking, requiring careful and thorough analysis of multiple data points (Dolence 1993). The outcome is not one enrollment goal, but many. Depending on institutional type, the goals will address a wide range of student attributes. Examples include:

- Academic ability
- Academic program interest
- Ethnicity
- Geographic origin
- Undergraduate/graduate
- Degree completion
- Distance education
- Financial status
- Resident status
- Program and facility capacities
- Special skills (fine arts, leadership, athletics)
- Religious affiliation

Setting enrollment goals at this level of detail is an intense and time-consuming process. This is where the link between institutional mission and student profile becomes apparent, as different campus stakeholders express their varying perspectives on which students the institution should enroll and why. Given the inherent difficulties, institutions often attempt to skip over this stage of planning and move quickly to implement tactics they believe will increase the number of students recruited or retained. However, the failure to take adequate time to develop foundational goals results in diminished results at each subsequent stage of the strategic planning process. Tactics tend to be deployed in an ad hoc, disjointed manner, with a failure to adequately account for the long-term implications for staff, financial resources, and other aspects of campus infrastructure. Staff and faculty charged with responsibility for recruitment and retention often burn out as they attempt to keep pace with a virtually endless list of activities that may have some merit, but are not prioritized and lack precision in addressing an ultimate set of desired enrollment outcomes. At best, institutions that operate in this manner spend extraordinary amounts of money to achieve modest enrollment increases that are short lived. In the worst cases, schools find themselves in a continual cycle of enrollment anxiety, with stagnant enrollment, regular budget shortfalls, and poor morale among campus stakeholders.

Developing comprehensive enrollment goals is best achieved through a process that commands institution-wide focus for three to six months, proceeding through the following steps.

- Appoint a SEM steering committee to guide the goal development process. This should be a group of faculty and staff with broad campus representation who possess interest in, commitment to, and operational awareness of recruitment and retention issues among all types of students enrolled at the institution.

  ▶ Review institutional mission to determine appropriate target student groups.

  ▶ Compile a table showing the enrollment history for each target student group over the past three to five years, calculating the percentage of each group in the overall student population.

  ▶ Develop *preliminary* enrollment goals, specifying the optimum percentage for each target student group, to be achieved over a ten-year period.[17]

  ▶ Identify priorities, indicating the order in which enrollment goals for specific target groups should be addressed. This acknowledges the reality that all goals for all target groups cannot be achieved simultaneously. Similarly, it recognizes that choices may need to be made among specific retention or recruitment activities in a particular year. Among the advantages of the ten-year planning period is the ability to focus on improving enrollment among one or two target groups or programs in years one and two of the plan, with other groups or programs receiving more focused attention in years four and five, and so forth.

---

[17] Crafting the preliminary goals should take into account institutional (e.g., personnel, programmatic, and physical capacities, governing mandates) and environmental (e.g., demographic, economic, and employment trends) factors. However, it is important to avoid the "paralysis by analysis" syndrome, in which many institutions find themselves poring over significant amounts of data while failing to move forward with enrollment planning and execution. The primary driver in the goal-setting process should be the desired future of the institution as reflected in mission-based goals, since most institutional and environmental factors can be addressed though targeted, strategic investments facilitated by the SEM Planning Model.

- The SEM steering committee gathers feedback and refines *preliminary* enrollment goals through campus-wide conversations.
  - ▶ Develop a presentation outlining the preliminary enrollment goals and priorities, and the rationale behind them.
  - ▶ Conduct a first round of campus conversations, including meetings with existing committees and groups, and convene open forums to encourage campus-wide participation.
  - ▶ Develop a *revised* list of enrollment goals and priorities.
  - ▶ Conduct a second round of campus conversations to gather feedback on the revised goals.
  - ▶ Develop a *recommended* list of enrollment goals and priorities.
- Submit *recommended* enrollment goals to the appropriate campus decision-making group, usually the chancellor's or president's cabinet, or equivalent group.
- The executive-level group determines what the final enrollment goals will be, either accepting the recommended goals or further refining them.
- Communicate the final enrollment goals to the campus and include them in formal planning documents and processes.
- Update goals every two to three years based on actual enrollment outcomes. The temptation to adjust the goals based on annual enrollment performance should be resisted except in the most obvious cases. Recruitment and retention initiatives often require at least two years to become fully operational and begin to influence student behavior. Among the core concepts of the SEM Planning Model is operating on the basis of longer-term trends, thereby avoiding knee-jerk reactions to short term outcomes.

## Phase 2:
### Identifying Strategic Enrollment Investments and Measureable Outcomes

The SEM Planning Model facilitates the creation of more effective investments in recruitment and retention initiatives. Increased effectiveness is achieved by:

- Accounting for the realistic costs associated with establishing new recruitment and retention initiatives;
- Creating realistic expectations regarding the time required for new initiatives to become established and influence students' enrollment behaviors for the long term;

- Identifying the specific enrollment outcomes expected as a result of recommended investments, allowing for objective evaluation of the performance of new enrollment initiatives; and
- Enabling informed decision-making on the continuation, alteration, or elimination of specific enrollment initiatives.

This phase generally requires the greatest change from traditional budgeting behavior. In the traditional approach, units that are asked to achieve higher-level recruitment and retention outcomes will generally assume that additional resources are required to do so, most often in the form of additional staff. There is a strong tendency to create a budget proposal that reads more like a wish list, based on the idea that the amount funded will be less than requested; therefore, the request should be higher in order to ensure that the amount ultimately allocated is adequate.

For their part, campus decision-makers and budget staff have traditionally assumed that budget requests for new enrollment initiatives will be inflated. There is a tendency to underestimate the effort and resources required to improve recruitment and retention results. Attention is focused on high-visibility tactics such as hiring additional recruiters, new marketing campaigns, or the latest technology enhancement. Less attention is given to more basic infrastructure needs that form the basis of sustainable enrollment results.

Often, in this paradigm, decisions are informed by anecdotal information, citing a story heard from one or a few students, or observing the success another institution had using a particular strategy. Many times goals are established with limited input from enrollment staff, allocating too few resources, and with unrealistic expectations. When new funds *are* allocated to boost enrollment, they tend to be one-time dispersals aimed at recruitment only and made available too late in the recruitment cycle to impact more than a few students.

In order for the SEM Planning Model to be effective, all involved must adopt a high level of budget discipline and collaboration. Units charged with recruitment and retention must be willing to rethink current business practices and enrollment strategies, giving as much attention to what they will stop doing as to the new strategies they will adopt. While there may ultimately be a need for additional staff, the first planning priority should be to look at ways of redeploying existing staff to address emerging needs and launch new initiatives. Enrollment units must be willing to put forth realistic budget requests that are not "padded," to be held accountable to measurable outcomes, and to shift course when targeted results are not met. Enrollment projections must be based on more than incremental increases over last year's numbers, taking into account hard data such as market share and specific gains associated with new initiatives.

At the same time, campus decision makers must be willing to collaborate closely with the enrollment professionals on their campus, recognizing the particular expertise associated with effective recruitment and retention work. Enrollment projections and budget decisions must be based on data, not anecdote, acknowledging the realistic investments required in order to achieve desired outcomes. The tendency to seek quick fix solutions and one-time allocations of funds must be avoided, recognizing the minimum twelve to eighteen months required to implement effective enrollment programs.

All involved must extend their planning horizon, understanding that efforts targeted to specific student populations, and the investments related to those efforts, will be deployed incrementally over the ten-year planning period. Operating in this manner runs counter to the egalitarian culture that exists in higher education. The reluctance to prioritize one student group, academic program, or departmental initiative over another is a major impediment to the type of planning described here. This is a primary reason for the extended, ten-year planning period – it allows for various campus constituents to see how and when their particular goals will be addressed. Whatever the challenges of prioritizing in the manner described here, the alternative is to flounder in an attempt to meet a set of ill-defined, over-broad goals. Among the main benefits of the SEM Planning Model is the clear communication of goals and priorities for all involved, leading to higher levels of alignment, efficiency, and success.

## Phase 3:
### Tracking Enrollment, Net Revenue and Institutional Budget Outcomes

Another shortcoming of traditional budgeting practices is the failure to track the net revenue resulting from enrollment investments. When funds are allocated to boost enrollment, actual enrollment outcomes often are not tracked in a systematic way, making it difficult to assess the return on investment.

The SEM Planning Model enables institutions to track net revenue by fully accounting for expenses and revenues associated with specific enrollment initiatives. With enrollment-related revenue accounting for the largest funding source for nearly every campus, this in turn facilitates more effective long-term budget planning at the institutional level.

### Phase 4:
### Creating Reinvestment Strategies

In traditional budgeting practice, new revenues resulting from enrollment increases are absorbed into the general fund. While all campus departments and personnel will benefit at some level from an improved bottom line at the institutional level, the potential positive impact of new monies is often lost in the "trickle down" approach. More likely, it will be observed that investments were made to specific departments to improve recruitment and retention, leaving others on campus to wonder "what's in it for me?" Virtually everyone who works in education maintains a value for assisting others to improve their lives; however, altruism only goes so far. The reality is that there are significant disincentives to increasing enrollment based on the simple fact that more students mean more work. Workload issues are most directly felt among teaching faculty, who have more exams and papers to grade, more meetings with students between class sessions, and so forth. In administrative units, modest increases in student numbers can be more easily absorbed through the use of student information systems and other technologies. However, with larger enrollment increases, even administrative units will begin to strain to keep up with the added workload.

The SEM Planning Model ameliorates the negative impacts of enrollment increases by clearly tracking the return on investments in enrollment initiatives, accounting for new revenues when they occur, and creating strategic reinvestment strategies that provide incentives and rewards for enrollment-enhancing efforts. Here again, prioritization and long-term planning is key. Efforts to allocate new revenue to all campus units in the first years of implementing the plan will be ineffectual, spreading funds too thinly to be of real value. Instead, the model allows institutions to demonstrate how various unit needs will be addressed over the course of the ten-year planning cycle, with higher-priority cohorts and needs being addressed in earlier years, and lower-priority—but still very important—areas receiving new funds in later years.

## IMPLEMENTING THE SEM PLANNING MODEL

The figures on the following pages illustrate how the planning approaches outlined above can be successfully integrated into a comprehensive institutional financial model. Though data in the example are fictitious and somewhat simplified, the financial relationships and implications of strategic decisions illustrated in this example are consistent with successful SEM implementations.

Table 5.1, on page 70, illustrates a sample format for a ten-year combined institutional enrollment and financial model at the highest summary level. Enrollments are noted at the beginning of each year, and SEM investments are noted in the expense section for each year. Upon its initial formulation, all variables in the model are flat-lined; that is, no enrollment, revenue, or expense increase or decrease assumptions are included for future years. As changes are introduced—additional enrollments, tuition increases, salary increases, or faculty additions, to cite some examples—the multi-year implications of those changes can be readily displayed. Note that the schedule also computes total costs per student and state appropriations (if applicable). A useful "companion" version of the schedule shown in Table 5.1 would display only the deltas (or changes) from year to year.

This summary "income statement" document is typical of how finances are viewed at an institutional level, and for enrollment plans to be expressed in terms of their impacts on institutional finances it is important to combine enrollment assumptions with revenue and expense projections, and also to include SEM costs as illustrated here.

In the goal-setting process, how enrollment variables are modeled and presented can be critical to establishing common understandings of the financial implications of alternative strategic enrollment decisions. Table 5.2, on page 72, illustrates one such presentation format that displays current revenues in total, specific subsets (described as "funnels") of overall enrollments (in this case out-of-state undergraduates are selected); the current distribution of enrollments for that subset by year or cohort which is important for projecting future enrollments; and resulting revenues, total enrollments, total tuition, and net tuition per student. The block below this summary provides the ability to change SEM variables for the selected funnel in each year (in this case, the number of matriculating students) and add investment costs associated with those changes.

**Table 5.1** ▶

SEM 10-Year
Planning Model

| | Budget (CY) | 1 | 2 | 3 |
|---|---|---|---|---|
| **ENROLLMENTS** | | | | |
| Prior Year Enrollment | 20,000 | 20,000 | 20,000 | 20,000 |
| Change (n) | | 0 | 0 | 0 |
| Total Enrollment ▶ | 20,000 | 20,000 | 20,000 | 20,000 |
| Change (%) | | 0 | 0 | 0 |
| **REVENUE** | | | | |
| State Appropriations for Instruction | 120,000,000 | 120,000,000 | 120,000,000 | 120,000,000 |
| Tuition and Enrollment Fees | 100,000,000 | 100,000,000 | 100,000,000 | 100,000,000 |
| Other Student Fees (General Education portion) | 20,000,000 | 20,000,000 | 20,000,000 | 20,000,000 |
| Other Education & General Revenues | 10,000,000 | 10,000,000 | 10,000,000 | 10,000,000 |
| Total Revenue ▶ | 250,000,000 | 250,000,000 | 250,000,000 | 250,000,000 |
| Change (%) | | 0 | 0 | 0 |
| **EXPENSE — Unit Budgets** | | | | |
| President | 8,889,821 | 8,889,821 | 8,889,821 | 8,889,821 |
| Provost — Colleges | | | | |
| College of Agricultural & Life Sciences | 23,677,583 | 23,677,583 | 23,677,583 | 23,677,583 |
| College of Art & Architecture | 9,752,816 | 9,752,816 | 9,752,816 | 9,752,816 |
| College of Business & Economics | 10,201,112 | 10,201,112 | 10,201,112 | 10,201,112 |
| College of Education | 11,933,649 | 11,933,649 | 11,933,649 | 11,933,649 |
| College of Engineering | 21,750,653 | 21,750,653 | 21,750,653 | 21,750,653 |
| College of Graduate Studies | 10,003,186 | 10,003,186 | 10,003,186 | 10,003,186 |
| College of Letters, Arts & Social Sciences | 11,705,532 | 11,705,532 | 11,705,532 | 11,705,532 |
| College of Natural Resources | 20,705,020 | 20,705,020 | 20,705,020 | 20,705,020 |
| College of Science | 7,091,008 | 7,091,008 | 7,091,008 | 7,091,008 |
| College of Veterinary Medicine | 1,856,535 | 1,856,535 | 1,856,535 | 1,856,535 |
| Educational Outreach | | | | |
| Remote Site 1 | 1,135,836 | 1,135,836 | 1,135,836 | 1,135,836 |
| Remote Site 2 | 596,666 | 596,666 | 596,666 | 596,666 |
| Remote Site 3 | 1,625,479 | 1,625,479 | 1,625,479 | 1,625,479 |
| Remote Site 4 | 410,935 | 410,935 | 410,935 | 410,935 |
| All Other Academic Programs | 3,953,913 | 3,953,913 | 3,953,913 | 3,953,913 |
| Central University | 33,253,822 | 33,253,822 | 33,253,822 | 33,253,822 |
| Finance & Administration | 38,126,356 | 38,126,356 | 38,126,356 | 38,126,356 |
| Fixed Costs | 4,419,292 | 4,419,292 | 4,419,292 | 4,419,292 |
| Student Affairs | 13,833,326 | 13,833,326 | 13,833,326 | 13,833,326 |
| University Advancement | 3,200,257 | 3,200,257 | 3,200,257 | 3,200,257 |
| University Research | 11,877,203 | 11,877,203 | 11,877,203 | 11,877,203 |
| Strategic Enrollment Management Costs | | 0 | 0 | 0 |
| Total Expense ▶ | 250,000,000 | 250,000,000 | 250,000,000 | 250,000,000 |
| Change (%) | 0 | 0 | 0 | 0 |
| Net of Operations ▶ | 0 | 0 | 0 | 0 |
| **Cumulative Surplus / (Shortfall)** | 0 | 0 | 0 | 0 |
| Educational & General Expense Per Student | 12,500 | 12,500 | 12,500 | 12,500 |
| State Appropriation Per Student | 6,000 | 6,000 | 6,000 | 6,000 |
| State Appropriation as % of Total E&G Expense | 48 | 48 | 48 | 48 |

| Plan Year | | | | | | | Change (%) |
|---|---|---|---|---|---|---|---|
| 4 | 5 | 6 | 7 | 8 | 9 | 10 | |
| 20,000 | 20,000 | 20,000 | 20,000 | 20,000 | 20,000 | 20,000 | |
| 0 | 0 | 0 | 0 | 0 | 0 | 0 | 0 |
| 20,000 | 20,000 | 20,000 | 20,000 | 20,000 | 20,000 | 20,000 | |
| 0 | 0 | 0 | 0 | 0 | 0 | 0 | 0 |
| | | | | | | | |
| 120,000,000 | 120,000,000 | 120,000,000 | 120,000,000 | 120,000,000 | 120,000,000 | 120,000,000 | |
| 100,000,000 | 100,000,000 | 100,000,000 | 100,000,000 | 100,000,000 | 100,000,000 | 100,000,000 | |
| 20,000,000 | 20,000,000 | 20,000,000 | 20,000,000 | 20,000,000 | 20,000,000 | 20,000,000 | |
| 10,000,000 | 10,000,000 | 10,000,000 | 10,000,000 | 10,000,000 | 10,000,000 | 10,000,000 | |
| 250,000,000 | 250,000,000 | 250,000,000 | 250,000,000 | 250,000,000 | 250,000,000 | 250,000,000 | |
| 0 | 0 | 0 | 0 | 0 | 0 | 0 | 0 |
| | | | | | | | |
| 8,889,821 | 8,889,821 | 8,889,821 | 8,889,821 | 8,889,821 | 8,889,821 | 8,889,821 | |
| | | | | | | | |
| 23,677,583 | 23,677,583 | 23,677,583 | 23,677,583 | 23,677,583 | 23,677,583 | 23,677,583 | |
| 9,752,816 | 9,752,816 | 9,752,816 | 9,752,816 | 9,752,816 | 9,752,816 | 9,752,816 | |
| 10,201,112 | 10,201,112 | 10,201,112 | 10,201,112 | 10,201,112 | 10,201,112 | 10,201,112 | |
| 11,933,649 | 11,933,649 | 11,933,649 | 11,933,649 | 11,933,649 | 11,933,649 | 11,933,649 | |
| 21,750,653 | 21,750,653 | 21,750,653 | 21,750,653 | 21,750,653 | 21,750,653 | 21,750,653 | |
| 10,003,186 | 10,003,186 | 10,003,186 | 10,003,186 | 10,003,186 | 10,003,186 | 10,003,186 | |
| 11,705,532 | 11,705,532 | 11,705,532 | 11,705,532 | 11,705,532 | 11,705,532 | 11,705,532 | |
| 20,705,020 | 20,705,020 | 20,705,020 | 20,705,020 | 20,705,020 | 20,705,020 | 20,705,020 | |
| 7,091,008 | 7,091,008 | 7,091,008 | 7,091,008 | 7,091,008 | 7,091,008 | 7,091,008 | |
| 1,856,535 | 1,856,535 | 1,856,535 | 1,856,535 | 1,856,535 | 1,856,535 | 1,856,535 | |
| | | | | | | | |
| 1,135,836 | 1,135,836 | 1,135,836 | 1,135,836 | 1,135,836 | 1,135,836 | 1,135,836 | |
| 596,666 | 596,666 | 596,666 | 596,666 | 596,666 | 596,666 | 596,666 | |
| 1,625,479 | 1,625,479 | 1,625,479 | 1,625,479 | 1,625,479 | 1,625,479 | 1,625,479 | |
| 410,935 | 410,935 | 410,935 | 410,935 | 410,935 | 410,935 | 410,935 | |
| 3,953,913 | 3,953,913 | 3,953,913 | 3,953,913 | 3,953,913 | 3,953,913 | 3,953,913 | |
| 33,253,822 | 33,253,822 | 33,253,822 | 33,253,822 | 33,253,822 | 33,253,822 | 33,253,822 | |
| 38,126,356 | 38,126,356 | 38,126,356 | 38,126,356 | 38,126,356 | 38,126,356 | 38,126,356 | |
| 4,419,292 | 4,419,292 | 4,419,292 | 4,419,292 | 4,419,292 | 4,419,292 | 4,419,292 | |
| 13,833,326 | 13,833,326 | 13,833,326 | 13,833,326 | 13,833,326 | 13,833,326 | 13,833,326 | |
| 3,200,257 | 3,200,257 | 3,200,257 | 3,200,257 | 3,200,257 | 3,200,257 | 3,200,257 | |
| 11,877,203 | 11,877,203 | 11,877,203 | 11,877,203 | 11,877,203 | 11,877,203 | 11,877,203 | |
| 0 | 0 | 0 | 0 | 0 | 0 | 0 | |
| 250,000,000 | 250,000,000 | 250,000,000 | 250,000,000 | 250,000,000 | 250,000,000 | 250,000,000 | |
| 0 | 0 | 0 | 0 | 0 | 0 | 0 | 0 |
| 0 | 0 | 0 | 0 | 0 | 0 | 0 | |
| **0** | **0** | **0** | **0** | **0** | **0** | **0** | |
| 12,500 | 12,500 | 12,500 | 12,500 | 12,500 | 12,500 | 12,500 | |
| 6,000 | 6,000 | 6,000 | 6,000 | 6,000 | 6,000 | 6,000 | |
| 48 | 48 | 48 | 48 | 48 | 48 | 48 | |

| | Current Year | 1 | 2 |
|---|---|---|---|
| **VARIABLES / STRATEGIES** | | | |
| Enrollment (Funnel = Undergraduate [Out Of State]) | | | |
| *Year 1* | 400 | 450 | 500 |
| *Year 2* | 300 | 300 | 338 |
| *Year 3* | 234 | 234 | 234 |
| *Year 4+* | 199 | 199 | 199 |
| Total Enrollments ▶ | 1,133 | 1,183 | 1,270 |
| First-Time, First-Year Matriculants | 400 | 435 | 470 |
| SEM Costs | | | |
| *Targeted Recruitment Activities — Nonresident Undergrads* | | 50,000 | 55,000 |
| *Enhanced Web Presence and Outreach* | | 25,000 | 27,500 |
| *New Student Scholarship ($2K / year for 4 years)* | | 100,000 | 274,000 |
| Total SEM Costs ▶ | | 175,000 | 356,500 |
| **RETURN ON INVESTMENT ANALYSIS (Thousands)** | | | |
| Post-Strategy Revenue | | 250,750.0 | 252,055.0 |
| Pre-Strategy Revenue | | 250,000.0 | 250,000.0 |
| Revenue Gain (Loss) | | 750.0 | 2,055.0 |
| Less Total SEM Costs | | (175.0) | (356.5) |
| **Net Gain (Loss)** | | **575.0** | **1,698.5** |
| ROI (%) | | 328.6 | 476.4 |
| Gross Revenue | 16,995,000 | 17,745,000 | 19,050,000 |
| Net Per Student | 15,000 | 14,852 | 14,719 |

**Table 5.2 ▶**

Revenues and Costs Associated With Strategy to Increase Out-of-State Undergraduate Enrollments

As discussed above, formulating specific enrollment goals and identifying costs associated with realizing those goals is critical to the SEM Planning Model. The institution in this example—a land-grant institution—has determined to increase its out-of-state undergraduate enrollments as a means of increasing revenues. This is certainly not an unusual strategy, as has been mentioned in preceding chapters, in the face of declining state support and higher tuition rates charged to nonresident students. The institution has decided to increase matriculants in this category by a modest number each year: fifty additional new entering students on a base of four hundred students per year. These students pay tuition of $15,000 per year, and no changes to persistence rates are assumed. In order to generate these additional fifty entering students, there are three separate strategies: "Targeted Recruitment Activities" at an initial annual cost of $50,000 and inflating 10 percent per year; "Enhanced Web Presence" at an initial annual cost of $25,000 and inflating 10 percent per year; and finally, a new scholarship program for each of the fifty new students

| Plan Year | | | | | | | |
|---|---|---|---|---|---|---|---|
| 3 | 4 | 5 | 6 | 7 | 8 | 9 | 10 |
| 550 | 600 | 650 | 700 | 750 | 800 | 850 | 900 |
| 375 | 413 | 450 | 488 | 525 | 563 | 600 | 638 |
| 263 | 293 | 322 | 351 | 380 | 410 | 439 | 468 |
| 199 | 224 | 249 | 273 | 298 | 323 | 348 | 373 |
| 1,387 | 1,529 | 1,670 | 1,812 | 1,954 | 2,095 | 2,237 | 2,378 |
| 505 | 540 | 575 | 610 | 645 | 680 | 715 | 750 |
| 60,500 | 66,550 | 73,205 | 80,526 | 88,578 | 97,436 | 107,179 | 117,897 |
| 30,250 | 33,275 | 36,603 | 40,263 | 44,289 | 48,718 | 53,590 | 58,949 |
| 508,000 | 792,000 | 1,074,000 | 1,358,000 | 1,642,000 | 1,924,000 | 2,208,000 | 2,490,000 |
| 598,750 | 891,825 | 1,183,808 | 1,478,788 | 1,774,867 | 2,070,154 | 2,368,769 | 2,666,846 |
| 253,810.0 | 255,940.0 | 258,055.0 | 260,185.0 | 262,315.0 | 264,430.0 | 266,560.0 | 268,675.0 |
| 250,000.0 | 250,000.0 | 250,000.0 | 250,000.0 | 250,000.0 | 250,000.0 | 250,000.0 | 250,000.0 |
| 3,810.0 | 5,940.0 | 8,055.0 | 10,185.0 | 12,315.0 | 14,430.0 | 16,560.0 | 18,675.0 |
| (598.8) | (891.8) | (1,183.8) | (1,478.8) | (1,774.9) | (2,070.2) | (2,368.8) | (2,666.8) |
| 3,211.3 | 5,048.2 | 6,871.2 | 8,706.2 | 10,540.1 | 12,359.8 | 14,191.2 | 16,008.2 |
| 536.3 | 566.1 | 580.4 | 588.7 | 265.2 | 265.2 | 265.2 | 265.2 |
| 20,805,000 | 22,935,000 | 25,050,000 | 27,180,000 | 29,310,000 | 31,425,000 | 33,555,000 | 35,670,000 |
| 14,568 | 14,417 | 14,291 | 14,184 | 14,092 | 14,012 | 13,941 | 13,879 |

providing a $2,000 annual scholarship for each new student. Of course specific strategies and the likelihood of their success vary considerably among different institutions; these are provided for illustrative purposes.

The return on investment block (bottom) of the schedule shows the financial outcomes of this combination of events. In the first year, gross revenues will increase by $750,000 and net revenues (after SEM costs) will increase $575,000. In the second year, gross revenues increase by $2,055,000 and net revenues by $1,698,500. By the tenth year these change assumptions are in place, gross revenues will have increased by $18,675,000 and net revenues by $16,008,200, with the difference of $2,666,800 invested in SEM activities and scholarships, and a total of 1,245 students will have been added to overall enrollments.

The next step is to integrate these outcomes into the institutional statement of revenues and expenses as shown in Table 5.3, on page 76. Note that this strategy results in enrollments increasing by 0.6 percent on average over the ten-year planning horizon; revenues increase by an average of 0.7 percent, and SEM expenses (the only incremental expense increases shown at this stage) add approximately 0.1 percent to total expenses. In terms of generating funds available for allocation to instructional programs and student, academic, and institutional support functions, this strategy yields a total of $79.2 million in net resources over the first ten years or approximately $16 million per year by its tenth year.

The budgetary allocation of these resources may follow institutional strategic priorities for a combination of instructional, research, student service, or infrastructure support needs. Whenever enrollment growth occurs, attention must be paid to maintaining the quality of current programs and services, and the extent to which there may be underutilized program or support capacity impacts the need for such investments. Combining all these considerations, the institution in the example may very well determine to phase in new faculty positions to maintain (or improve) its student to faculty ratio, increase institutionally funded financial aid, or make similar investments to achieve its institutional mission. Whatever these institutional investment decisions may be, identifying growth opportunities using this planning approach has plainly quantified the future resources available to fund those investments.

At this budget allocation stage many essential costs such as salary and benefit inflation, plant operation and maintenance, and similar costs would also be added. Additionally, some assumptions regarding tuition rate increases and possibly other revenue increases would be inserted. In Table 5.4, on page 78, allocations of the new net revenues have simply been allocated on a pro rata basis across all areas of the institution including SEM investments. Note that the total education and general funding per student increases overall based on this strategy alone prior to any other revenue increases, as enrollments for students paying higher than average tuition rates are increasing.

## USING THE SEM PLANNING MODEL TO EVALUATE SPECIFIC INITIATIVES

Table 5.5, on page 80, illustrates the modeling of enrollments and net revenues associated with the introduction of a freshman seminar anticipated to cost $100,000 per year and projected to improve in-state (or resident) undergraduate first to second year retention by 0.5 percent. In the first year of the strategy there are costs but no change in retention. Consequently in the "return on investment" section revenues are unchanged compared to "pre-strategy revenues," yet expenses are higher, resulting in a net loss of $100,000. In Plan Year 2, the second year of the strategy, the 0.5 percent increase in persistence has resulted in ten additional students compared to the prior year or a revenue gain of $50,000; however, the strategy still generates a net loss of $50,000 in year two. In Plan Year 4, with three years of resulting enrollment increases in the pipeline, this strategy yields some net revenue. By Plan Year 7 enrollments stabilize at a level approximately thirty-one FTE higher than in the current year, with net revenues of $55,000 per year assuming no costs beyond those for the seminar.

This form of analysis facilitates numerous helpful enrollment management discussions and above all establishes the clear linkages between strategic investment decisions and likely outcomes, both financial and nonfinancial. In the example, an argument could be made that a 0.5 percent persistence increase does not merit this level of investment—perhaps alternative strategies could yield more significant outcomes. Of course the 0.5 percent assumption may be artificially low; the experience of other institutions with similar strategies is helpful in setting up such parameters.

The fundamental mathematical fact that it takes *seven years* for the consequences of this strategy to play out is itself significant. As noted above and in preceding chapters, institutional budget decisions tend to focus on the "here and now" and long-term follow up on investments made the better part of a decade ago is not a strength of college and university budgeting. Yet the reality of enrollment strategies, when time to graduation averages five years, will be, consistently, that their full impact will not be known for five to seven years depending on the nature of the strategy.

Scholarship and financial aid leveraging initiatives can be modeled in a similar fashion to demonstrate or evaluate the efficacy of alternative programs. Table 5.6, on page 82, is an example showing the revenues and expenses associated with a multi-year "persistence scholarship" designed to attract students from an unrepresented market segment (and consequently adding to total enrollments). The scholarship program awards $1,000 to students who persist from year one to year two; $2,000 for those persisting from year two to year three; and $3,000 for year three to year four. Assuming 90 percent persistence rates in each year, the gross revenues and scholarship expenses are as shown for entering cohorts of one hundred students per year.

Table 5.3 ▶

Allocable Net
Revenues Resulting
from SEM Strategy

| | Budget (CY) | 1 | 2 | 3 |
|---|---|---|---|---|
| **ENROLLMENTS** | | | | |
| Prior Year Enrollment | 20,000 | 20,000 | 20,050 | 20,137 |
| Enrollment Change | 0 | 50 | 87 | 117 |
| Total Enrollment ▶ | 20,000 | 20,050 | 20,137 | 20,254 |
| Change (%) | — | 0.3 | 0.4 | 0.6 |
| **REVENUE** | | | | |
| State Appropriations for Instruction | 120,000,000 | 120,000,000 | 120,000,000 | 120,000,000 |
| Tuition and Enrollment Fees | 100,000,000 | 100,750,000 | 102,055,000 | 103,810,000 |
| Other Student Fees (General Education portion) | 20,000,000 | 20,000,000 | 20,000,000 | 20,000,000 |
| Other Education & General Revenues | 10,000,000 | 10,000,000 | 10,000,000 | 10,000,000 |
| Total Revenue ▶ | 250,000,000 | 250,750,000 | 252,055,000 | 253,810,000 |
| Change (%) | — | 0.3 | 0.5 | 0.7 |
| **EXPENSE — Unit Budgets** | | | | |
| President | 8,889,821 | 8,889,821 | 8,889,821 | 8,889,821 |
| Provost — Colleges | | | | |
| *College of Agricultural & Life Sciences* | 23,677,583 | 23,677,583 | 23,677,583 | 23,677,583 |
| *College of Art & Architecture* | 9,752,816 | 9,752,816 | 9,752,816 | 9,752,816 |
| *College of Business & Economics* | 10,201,112 | 10,201,112 | 10,201,112 | 10,201,112 |
| *College of Education* | 11,933,649 | 11,933,649 | 11,933,649 | 11,933,649 |
| *College of Engineering* | 21,750,653 | 21,750,653 | 21,750,653 | 21,750,653 |
| *College of Graduate Studies* | 10,003,186 | 10,003,186 | 10,003,186 | 10,003,186 |
| *College of Letters, Arts & Social Sciences* | 11,705,532 | 11,705,532 | 11,705,532 | 11,705,532 |
| *College of Natural Resources* | 20,705,020 | 20,705,020 | 20,705,020 | 20,705,020 |
| *College of Science* | 7,091,008 | 7,091,008 | 7,091,008 | 7,091,008 |
| *College of Veterinary Medicine* | 1,856,535 | 1,856,535 | 1,856,535 | 1,856,535 |
| Educational Outreach | | | | |
| *Remote Site 1* | 1,135,836 | 1,135,836 | 1,135,836 | 1,135,836 |
| *Remote Site 2* | 596,666 | 596,666 | 596,666 | 596,666 |
| *Remote Site 3* | 1,625,479 | 1,625,479 | 1,625,479 | 1,625,479 |
| *Remote Site 4* | 410,935 | 410,935 | 410,935 | 410,935 |
| All Other Academic Programs | 3,953,913 | 3,953,913 | 3,953,913 | 3,953,913 |
| Central University | 33,253,822 | 33,253,822 | 33,253,822 | 33,253,822 |
| Finance & Administration | 38,126,356 | 38,126,356 | 38,126,356 | 38,126,356 |
| Fixed Costs | 4,419,292 | 4,419,292 | 4,419,292 | 4,419,292 |
| Student Affairs | 13,833,326 | 13,833,326 | 13,833,326 | 13,833,326 |
| University Advancement | 3,200,257 | 3,200,257 | 3,200,257 | 3,200,257 |
| University Research | 11,877,203 | 11,877,203 | 11,877,203 | 11,877,203 |
| Strategic Enrollment Management Costs | | 175,000 | 356,500 | 598,750 |
| Total Expense ▶ | 250,000,000 | 250,175,000 | 250,356,500 | 250,598,750 |
| Change (%) | — | 0.1 | 0.1 | 0.1 |
| Net Of Operations ▶ | 0 | 575,000 | 1,698,500 | 3,211,250 |
| **Cumulative Surplus / (Shortfall)** | **0** | **575,000** | **2,273,500** | **5,484,750** |
| Educational & General Expense Per Student: | 12,500 | 12,478 | 12,433 | 12,373 |
| State Appropriation Per Student: | 6,000 | 5,985 | 5,959 | 5,925 |
| State Appropriation as % of Total E&G Expense: | 48.0 | 47.9 | 47.6 | 47.3 |

| Plan Year | | | | | | | Change (%) |
|---|---|---|---|---|---|---|---|
| 4 | 5 | 6 | 7 | 8 | 9 | 10 | |
| 20,254 | 20,396 | 20,537 | 20,679 | 20,821 | 20,962 | 21,104 | |
| 142 | 141 | 142 | 142 | 141 | 142 | 141 | |
| 20,396 | 20,537 | 20,679 | 20,821 | 20,962 | 21,104 | 21,245 | |
| 0.7 | 0.7 | 0.7 | 0.7 | 0.7 | 0.7 | 0.7 | 0.6 |
| | | | | | | | |
| 120,000,000 | 120,000,000 | 120,000,000 | 120,000,000 | 120,000,000 | 120,000,000 | 120,000,000 | |
| 105,940,000 | 108,055,000 | 110,185,000 | 112,315,000 | 114,430,000 | 116,560,000 | 118,675,000 | |
| 20,000,000 | 20,000,000 | 20,000,000 | 20,000,000 | 20,000,000 | 20,000,000 | 20,000,000 | |
| 10,000,000 | 10,000,000 | 10,000,000 | 10,000,000 | 10,000,000 | 10,000,000 | 10,000,000 | |
| 255,940,000 | 258,055,000 | 260,185,000 | 262,315,000 | 264,430,000 | 266,560,000 | 268,675,000 | |
| 0.8 | 0.8 | 0.8 | 0.8 | 0.8 | 0.8 | 0.8 | 0.7 |
| | | | | | | | |
| 8,889,821 | 8,889,821 | 8,889,821 | 8,889,821 | 8,889,821 | 8,889,821 | 8,889,821 | |
| | | | | | | | |
| 23,677,583 | 23,677,583 | 23,677,583 | 23,677,583 | 23,677,583 | 23,677,583 | 23,677,583 | |
| 9,752,816 | 9,752,816 | 9,752,816 | 9,752,816 | 9,752,816 | 9,752,816 | 9,752,816 | |
| 10,201,112 | 10,201,112 | 10,201,112 | 10,201,112 | 10,201,112 | 10,201,112 | 10,201,112 | |
| 11,933,649 | 11,933,649 | 11,933,649 | 11,933,649 | 11,933,649 | 11,933,649 | 11,933,649 | |
| 21,750,653 | 21,750,653 | 21,750,653 | 21,750,653 | 21,750,653 | 21,750,653 | 21,750,653 | |
| 10,003,186 | 10,003,186 | 10,003,186 | 10,003,186 | 10,003,186 | 10,003,186 | 10,003,186 | |
| 11,705,532 | 11,705,532 | 11,705,532 | 11,705,532 | 11,705,532 | 11,705,532 | 11,705,532 | |
| 20,705,020 | 20,705,020 | 20,705,020 | 20,705,020 | 20,705,020 | 20,705,020 | 20,705,020 | |
| 7,091,008 | 7,091,008 | 7,091,008 | 7,091,008 | 7,091,008 | 7,091,008 | 7,091,008 | |
| 1,856,535 | 1,856,535 | 1,856,535 | 1,856,535 | 1,856,535 | 1,856,535 | 1,856,535 | |
| | | | | | | | |
| 1,135,836 | 1,135,836 | 1,135,836 | 1,135,836 | 1,135,836 | 1,135,836 | 1,135,836 | |
| 596,666 | 596,666 | 596,666 | 596,666 | 596,666 | 596,666 | 596,666 | |
| 1,625,479 | 1,625,479 | 1,625,479 | 1,625,479 | 1,625,479 | 1,625,479 | 1,625,479 | |
| 410,935 | 410,935 | 410,935 | 410,935 | 410,935 | 410,935 | 410,935 | |
| 3,953,913 | 3,953,913 | 3,953,913 | 3,953,913 | 3,953,913 | 3,953,913 | 3,953,913 | |
| 33,253,822 | 33,253,822 | 33,253,822 | 33,253,822 | 33,253,822 | 33,253,822 | 33,253,822 | |
| 38,126,356 | 38,126,356 | 38,126,356 | 38,126,356 | 38,126,356 | 38,126,356 | 38,126,356 | |
| 4,419,292 | 4,419,292 | 4,419,292 | 4,419,292 | 4,419,292 | 4,419,292 | 4,419,292 | |
| 13,833,326 | 13,833,326 | 13,833,326 | 13,833,326 | 13,833,326 | 13,833,326 | 13,833,326 | |
| 3,200,257 | 3,200,257 | 3,200,257 | 3,200,257 | 3,200,257 | 3,200,257 | 3,200,257 | |
| 11,877,203 | 11,877,203 | 11,877,203 | 11,877,203 | 11,877,203 | 11,877,203 | 11,877,203 | |
| 891,825 | 1,183,808 | 1,478,788 | 1,774,867 | 2,070,154 | 2,368,769 | 2,666,846 | |
| 250,891,825 | 251,183,808 | 251,478,788 | 251,774,867 | 252,070,154 | 252,368,769 | 252,666,846 | |
| 0.1 | 0.1 | 0.1 | 0.1 | 0.1 | 0.1 | 0.1 | 0.1 |
| 5,048,175 | 6,871,193 | 8,706,212 | 10,540,133 | 12,359,846 | 14,191,231 | 16,008,154 | |
| 10,532,925 | 17,404,118 | 26,110,329 | 36,650,462 | 49,010,308 | 63,201,539 | 79,209,693 | |
| | | | | | | | |
| 12,301 | 12,231 | 12,161 | 12,092 | 12,025 | 11,958 | 11,893 | |
| 5,884 | 5,843 | 5,803 | 5,763 | 5,725 | 5,686 | 5,648 | |
| 46.9 | 46.5 | 46.1 | 45.7 | 45.4 | 45.0 | 44.7 | |

**Table 5.4** ►

Pro Rata Distribution
of Net Revenues

| | Budget (CY) | 1 | 2 | 3 |
|---|---|---|---|---|
| **ENROLLMENTS** | | | | |
| Prior Year Enrollment | 20,000 | 20,000 | 20,050 | 20,137 |
| Enrollment Change | 0 | 50 | 87 | 117 |
| Total Enrollment ► | 20,000 | 20,050 | 20,137 | 20,254 |
| Change (%) | | 0.3 | 0.4 | 0.6 |
| **REVENUE** | | | | |
| State Appropriations for Instruction | 120,000,000 | 120,000,000 | 120,000,000 | 120,000,000 |
| Tuition and Enrollment Fees | 100,000,000 | 100,750,000 | 102,055,000 | 103,810,000 |
| Other Student Fees (General Education portion) | 20,000,000 | 20,000,000 | 20,000,000 | 20,000,000 |
| Other Education & General Revenues | 10,000,000 | 10,000,000 | 10,000,000 | 10,000,000 |
| Total Revenue ► | 250,000,000 | 250,750,000 | 252,055,000 | 253,810,000 |
| Change (%) | | 0.3 | 0.5 | 0.7 |
| **EXPENSE — Unit Budgets** | | | | |
| President | 8,889,821 | 8,910,253 | 8,950,132 | 9,003,738 |
| Provost — Colleges | | | | |
| *College of Agricultural & Life Sciences* | 23,677,583 | 23,732,004 | 23,838,220 | 23,980,995 |
| *College of Art & Architecture* | 9,752,816 | 9,775,232 | 9,818,982 | 9,877,792 |
| *College of Business & Economics* | 10,201,112 | 10,224,558 | 10,270,320 | 10,331,832 |
| *College of Education* | 11,933,649 | 11,961,077 | 12,014,611 | 12,086,570 |
| *College of Engineering* | 21,750,653 | 21,800,644 | 21,898,216 | 22,029,372 |
| *College of Graduate Studies* | 10,003,186 | 10,026,177 | 10,071,051 | 10,131,370 |
| *College of Letters, Arts & Social Sciences* | 11,705,532 | 11,732,436 | 11,784,946 | 11,855,530 |
| *College of Natural Resources* | 20,705,020 | 20,752,608 | 20,845,489 | 20,970,340 |
| *College of Science* | 7,091,008 | 7,107,306 | 7,139,116 | 7,181,874 |
| *College of Veterinary Medicine* | 1,856,535 | 1,860,802 | 1,869,131 | 1,880,325 |
| Educational Outreach | | | | |
| *Remote Site 1* | 1,135,836 | 1,138,447 | 1,143,542 | 1,150,391 |
| *Remote Site 2* | 596,666 | 598,038 | 600,714 | 604,312 |
| *Remote Site 3* | 1,625,479 | 1,629,215 | 1,636,507 | 1,646,309 |
| *Remote Site 4* | 410,935 | 411,879 | 413,723 | 416,201 |
| All Other Academic Programs | 3,953,913 | 3,963,001 | 3,980,738 | 4,004,580 |
| Central University | 33,253,822 | 33,330,252 | 33,479,427 | 33,679,947 |
| Finance & Administration | 38,126,356 | 38,213,986 | 38,385,018 | 38,614,919 |
| Fixed Costs | 4,419,292 | 4,429,449 | 4,449,274 | 4,475,922 |
| Student Affairs | 13,833,326 | 13,865,120 | 13,927,176 | 14,010,591 |
| University Advancement | 3,200,257 | 3,207,612 | 3,221,969 | 3,241,266 |
| University Research | 11,877,203 | 11,904,501 | 11,957,781 | 12,029,401 |
| Strategic Enrollment Management Costs | | 175,402 | 358,919 | 606,423 |
| Total Expense ► | 250,000,000 | 250,750,000 | 252,055,000 | 253,810,000 |
| Change (%) | | 0.3 | 0.5 | 0.7 |
| Net of Operations ► | 0 | 0 | 0 | 0 |
| **Cumulative Surplus / (Shortfall)** | **0** | **0** | **0** | **0** |
| Educational & General Expense Per Student: | 12,500 | 12,506 | 12,517 | 12,531 |
| State Appropriation Per Student: | 6,000 | 5,985 | 5,959 | 5,925 |
| State Appropriation as of Total E&G Expense: | 48.0 | 47.9 | 47.6 | 47.3 |

| Plan Year | | | | | | | Change (%) |
|---|---|---|---|---|---|---|---|
| 4 | 5 | 6 | 7 | 8 | 9 | 10 | |
| 20,254 | 20,396 | 20,537 | 20,679 | 20,821 | 20,962 | 21,104 | |
| 142 | 141 | 142 | 142 | 141 | 142 | 141 | |
| 20,396 | 20,537 | 20,679 | 20,821 | 20,962 | 21,104 | 21,245 | |
| 0.7 | 0.7 | 0.7 | 0.7 | 0.7 | 0.7 | 0.7 | 0.6 |
| | | | | | | | |
| 120,000,000 | 120,000,000 | 120,000,000 | 120,000,000 | 120,000,000 | 120,000,000 | 120,000,000 | |
| 105,940,000 | 108,055,000 | 110,185,000 | 112,315,000 | 114,430,000 | 116,560,000 | 118,675,000 | |
| 20,000,000 | 20,000,000 | 20,000,000 | 20,000,000 | 20,000,000 | 20,000,000 | 20,000,000 | |
| 10,000,000 | 10,000,000 | 10,000,000 | 10,000,000 | 10,000,000 | 10,000,000 | 10,000,000 | |
| 255,940,000 | 258,055,000 | 260,185,000 | 262,315,000 | 264,430,000 | 266,560,000 | 268,675,000 | |
| 0.8 | 0.8 | 0.8 | 0.8 | 0.8 | 0.8 | 0.8 | 0.7 |
| | | | | | | | |
| 9,068,692 | 9,133,004 | 9,197,587 | 9,261,978 | 9,325,719 | 9,389,714 | 9,453,051 | |
| | | | | | | | |
| 24,153,998 | 24,325,289 | 24,497,303 | 24,668,806 | 24,838,575 | 25,009,024 | 25,177,718 | |
| 9,949,052 | 10,019,607 | 10,090,459 | 10,161,101 | 10,231,029 | 10,301,238 | 10,370,723 | |
| 10,406,368 | 10,480,166 | 10,554,275 | 10,628,164 | 10,701,307 | 10,774,742 | 10,847,421 | |
| 12,173,765 | 12,260,097 | 12,346,792 | 12,433,231 | 12,518,796 | 12,604,703 | 12,689,726 | |
| 22,188,296 | 22,345,647 | 22,503,661 | 22,661,207 | 22,817,160 | 22,973,738 | 23,128,703 | |
| 10,204,459 | 10,276,825 | 10,349,497 | 10,421,953 | 10,493,676 | 10,565,686 | 10,636,955 | |
| 11,941,058 | 12,025,739 | 12,110,778 | 12,195,564 | 12,279,493 | 12,363,759 | 12,447,157 | |
| 21,121,624 | 21,271,410 | 21,421,829 | 21,571,801 | 21,720,256 | 21,869,307 | 22,016,823 | |
| 7,233,685 | 7,284,984 | 7,336,499 | 7,387,861 | 7,438,704 | 7,489,750 | 7,540,271 | |
| 1,893,890 | 1,907,321 | 1,920,809 | 1,934,256 | 1,947,567 | 1,960,932 | 1,974,159 | |
| | | | | | | | |
| 1,158,690 | 1,166,907 | 1,175,159 | 1,183,386 | 1,191,530 | 1,199,707 | 1,207,799 | |
| 608,672 | 612,988 | 617,323 | 621,645 | 625,923 | 630,218 | 634,469 | |
| 1,658,185 | 1,669,945 | 1,681,753 | 1,693,527 | 1,705,182 | 1,716,883 | 1,728,464 | |
| 419,203 | 422,176 | 425,161 | 428,138 | 431,084 | 434,042 | 436,970 | |
| 4,033,470 | 4,062,073 | 4,090,798 | 4,119,437 | 4,147,787 | 4,176,250 | 4,204,420 | |
| 33,922,919 | 34,163,488 | 34,405,071 | 34,645,937 | 34,884,368 | 35,123,755 | 35,360,676 | |
| 38,893,494 | 39,169,312 | 39,446,293 | 39,722,452 | 39,995,820 | 40,270,282 | 40,541,919 | |
| 4,508,212 | 4,540,183 | 4,572,288 | 4,604,298 | 4,635,985 | 4,667,798 | 4,699,284 | |
| 14,111,665 | 14,211,740 | 14,312,237 | 14,412,435 | 14,511,620 | 14,611,203 | 14,709,761 | |
| 3,264,649 | 3,287,801 | 3,311,050 | 3,334,230 | 3,357,176 | 3,380,214 | 3,403,015 | |
| 12,116,183 | 12,202,106 | 12,288,392 | 12,374,422 | 12,459,582 | 12,545,083 | 12,629,704 | |
| 909,769 | 1,216,191 | 1,529,984 | 1,849,169 | 2,171,660 | 2,501,970 | 2,835,809 | |
| 255,940,000 | 258,055,000 | 260,185,000 | 262,315,000 | 264,430,000 | 266,560,000 | 268,675,000 | |
| 0.8 | 0.8 | 0.8 | 0.8 | 0.8 | 0.8 | 0.8 | 0.7 |
| 0 | 0 | 0 | 0 | 0 | 0 | 0 | |
| 0 | 0 | 0 | 0 | 0 | 0 | 0 | |
| 12,549 | 12,565 | 12,582 | 12,599 | 12,615 | 12,631 | 12,647 | |
| 5,884 | 5,843 | 5,803 | 5,763 | 5,725 | 5,686 | 5,648 | |
| 46.9 | 46.5 | 46.1 | 45.7 | 45.4 | 45.0 | 44.7 | |

| | Current Year | 1 | 2 |
|---|---|---|---|
| **VARIABLES / STRATEGIES** | | | |
| Enrollment (Funnel = UNDERGRADUATE [In-State]) | | | |
| _Year 1_ | 2,000 | 2,000 | 2,000 |
| _Year 2_ | 1,710 | 1,710 | 1,720 |
| _Year 3_ | 1,368 | 1,368 | 1,368 |
| _Year 4+_ | 2,188 | 2,188 | 2,188 |
| Total Enrollments ▶ | 7,266 | 7,266 | 7,276 |
| Year 1 to Year 2 Persistence Rate (%) | 85.5 | 85.5 | 86.0 |
| SEM Costs | | | |
| _Introduce Freshman Seminar_ | | 100,000 | 100,000 |
| Total SEM Costs ▶ | | 100,000 | 100,000 |
| **RETURN ON INVESTMENT ANALYSIS (Thousands)** | | | |
| Post-Strategy Revenue | | 250,000.0 | 250,050.0 |
| Pre-Strategy Revenue | | 250,000.0 | 250,000.0 |
| Revenue Gain (loss) | | —- | 50.0 |
| Less Total SEM Costs | | (100.0) | (100.0) |
| **Net Gain (Loss)** | | **(100.0)** | **(50.0)** |
| ROI (%) | | -100.0 | -50.0 |
| Gross Revenue | 36,330,000 | 36,330,000 | 36,380,000 |
| Net Per Student | 5,000 | 4,986 | 4,986 |

For budget planning purposes, some level of precision (or high level probabilities) in revenue projections is critical. The example in Figure 5.6 anticipates about 344 additional student FTEs by the time this program is fully implemented. It is possible in a very large institution that such an enrollment increase would not require many, if any, additional faculty or student support resources. Yet, at many institutions an enrollment increase of this magnitude would require significant instructional, academic support, and perhaps even institutional support investments. The analytical framework of the SEM Planning Model provides the kind of detailed budgetary information not only to support such decision making, but to facilitate detailed planning concerning possible levels of investments or estimating what support requirements might arise over a given planning horizon. Speaking of 344 additional students "next year" is much different than a phased transition over multiple years; quantifying such transitions makes possible appropriate academic and even any necessary facility or support services planning.

| Plan Year | | | | | | | |
|---|---|---|---|---|---|---|---|
| 3 | 4 | 5 | 6 | 7 | 8 | 9 | 10 |
| 2,000 | 2,000 | 2,000 | 2,000 | 2,000 | 2,000 | 2,000 | 2,000 |
| 1,720 | 1,720 | 1,720 | 1,720 | 1,720 | 1,720 | 1,720 | 1,720 |
| 1,376 | 1,376 | 1,376 | 1,376 | 1,376 | 1,376 | 1,376 | 1,376 |
| 2,188 | 2,195 | 2,198 | 2,200 | 2,201 | 2,201 | 2,201 | 2,201 |
| 7,284 | 7,291 | 7,294 | 7,296 | 7,297 | 7,297 | 7,297 | 7,297 |
| 86.0 | 86.0 | 86.0 | 86.0 | 86.0 | 86.0 | 86.0 | 86.0 |
| 100,000 | 100,000 | 100,000 | 100,000 | 100,000 | 100,000 | 100,000 | 100,000 |
| 100,000 | 100,000 | 100,000 | 100,000 | 100,000 | 100,000 | 100,000 | 100,000 |
| 250,090.0 | 250,125.0 | 250,140.0 | 250,150.0 | 250,155.0 | 250,155.0 | 250,155.0 | 250,155.0 |
| 250,000.0 | 250,000.0 | 250,000.0 | 250,000.0 | 250,000.0 | 250,000.0 | 250,000.0 | 250,000.0 |
| 90.0 | 125.0 | 140.0 | 150.0 | 155.0 | 155.0 | 155.0 | 155.0 |
| (100.0) | (100.0) | (100.0) | (100.0) | (100.0) | (100.0) | (100.0) | (100.0) |
| (10.0) | 25.0 | 40.0 | 50.0 | 55.0 | 55.0 | 55.0 | 55.0 |
| -10.0 | 25.0 | 40.0 | 50.0 | 55.0 | 55.0 | 55.0 | 55.0 |
| 36,420,000 | 36,455,000 | 36,470,000 | 36,480,000 | 36,485,000 | 36,485,000 | 36,485,000 | 36,485,000 |
| 4,986 | 4,986 | 4,986 | 4,986 | 4,986 | 4,986 | 4,986 | 4,986 |

Finally, when openly shared in a transparent fashion such as this, all participants in the planning process gain some level of ownership in the resulting SEM plan and the investments and reinvestments these plans may call for. New avenues of collaboration open up for SEM managers when academic constituencies (faculty) see the financial implications of retention and recruitment activities and the direct relationship between retention, recruitment, and funds available to support salaries and programs. Similarly, when institutional financial planners clearly see the linkages between SEM investments and the revenue generation supporting the institution overall—and the relatively lengthy timeframe for those investments to fully play out—the result is new levels of due process for funding proposals associated with SEM initiatives.

## SUMMARY

The SEM Planning Model offers a new approach to enrollment and institutional budget planning. By bringing together comprehensive enrollment goals, strategic

Table 5.6 ▶

Modeling Impact of a
Scholarship Program

| | | Current Year | 1 | 2 |
|---|---|---|---|---|
| **VARIABLES / STRATEGIES** | | | | |
| Enrollment (Funnell = Specialty Funnel 1 [In-State UG]) | | | | |
| *Year 1* | | — | 100 | 100 |
| *Year 2* | | — | — | 90 |
| *Year 3* | | — | — | — |
| *Year 4+* | | — | — | — |
| **Total Enrollments ▶** | | — | 100 | 190 |
| Year 1 to Year 3 Persistence Rate (%) | | — | 90.0 | 90.0 |
| SEM Costs | | | | |
| *First year persistence scholarship — $1K* | | | | 90,000 |
| *Second year persistence scholarship — $2K* | | | | 0 |
| *Third year persistence scholarship — $3K* | | | | 0 |
| **Total SEM Costs ▶** | | | — | 90,000 |
| **RETURN ON INVESTMENT ANALYSIS (Thousands)** | | | | |
| Post-Strategy Revenue | | | 250,500.0 | 250,950.0 |
| Pre-Strategy Revenue | | | 250,000.0 | 250,000.0 |
| Revenue Gain (loss) | | | 500.0 | 950.0 |
| Less Total SEM Costs | | | — | (90.0) |
| **Net Gain (loss)** | | | **500.0** | **860.0** |
| ROI (%) | | | — | 955.6 |
| Gross Revenue | | — | 500,000 | 950,000 |
| Net Per Student | | — | 5,000 | 4,526 |

enrollment investments, measurable enrollment outcomes, net revenue results, institutional budget outcomes, and strategic reinvestment strategies, the model can help institutions make better informed and more effective financial decisions. At least as important are the collateral benefits the model offers. By bringing new levels of transparency to enrollment goals and outcomes, this Model fosters greater trust among campus stakeholders, and enables them to see more clearly the implications of institutional decisions on student access and success. The benefits of this approach offer hope improving outcomes not only at the institutional level, but for American higher education as a whole.

| | Plan Year | | | | | | | |
|---|---|---|---|---|---|---|---|---|
| 3 | 4 | 5 | 6 | 7 | 8 | 9 | 10 |
| 100 | 100 | 100 | 100 | 100 | 100 | 100 | 100 |
| 90 | 90 | 90 | 90 | 90 | 90 | 90 | 90 |
| 81 | 81 | 81 | 81 | 81 | 81 | 81 | 81 |
| — | — | 73 | 73 | 73 | 73 | 73 | 73 |
| 271 | 344 | 344 | 344 | 344 | 344 | 344 | 344 |
| 90.0 | 90.0 | 90.0 | 90.0 | 90.0 | 90.0 | 90.0 | 90.0 |
| | | | | | | | |
| 90,000 | 90,000 | 90,000 | 90,000 | 90,000 | 90,000 | 90,000 | 90,000 |
| 162,000 | 162,000 | 162,000 | 162,000 | 162,000 | 162,000 | 162,000 | 162,000 |
| 0 | 219,000 | 219,000 | 219,000 | 219,000 | 219,000 | 219,000 | 219,000 |
| 252,000 | 471,000 | 471,000 | 471,000 | 471,000 | 471,000 | 471,000 | 471,000 |
| | | | | | | | |
| 251,355.0 | 251,720.0 | 251,720.0 | 251,720.0 | 251,720.0 | 251,720.0 | 251,720.0 | 251,720.0 |
| 250,000.0 | 250,000.0 | 250,000.0 | 250,000.0 | 250,000.0 | 250,000.0 | 250,000.0 | 250,000.0 |
| 1,355.0 | 1,720.0 | 1,720.0 | 1,720.0 | 1,720.0 | 1,720.0 | 1,720.0 | 1,720.0 |
| (252.0) | (471.0) | (471.0) | (471.0) | (471.0) | (471.0) | (471.0) | (471.0) |
| 1,103.0 | 1,249.0 | 1,249.0 | 1,249.0 | 1,249.0 | 1,249.0 | 1,249.0 | 1,249.0 |
| 437.7 | 265.2 | 265.2 | 265.2 | 265.2 | 265.2 | 265.2 | 265.2 |
| | | | | | | | |
| 1,355,000 | 1,720,000 | 1,720,000 | 1,720,000 | 1,720,000 | 1,720,000 | 1,720,000 | 1,720,000 |
| 4,070 | 3,631 | 3,631 | 3,631 | 3,631 | 3,631 | 3,631 | 3,631 |

CHAPTER SIX
*by* BOB BONTRAGER

# 6

# The Enrollment Leadership Imperative

The need for change in the delivery of American higher education has been well documented. A recent representative report in *Inside Higher Education* (2008) details a discussion of this issue where educators and public education officials concluded that "states may need to change their methods for funding colleges to... reward institutions that educate large numbers of needy undergraduate students and focus less on research, for instance, the sort of shift that is likely to mean re-distributing money away from institutions (elite flagships, for instance) that are accustomed to getting lots of it." The group went on to call for a fundamental re-structuring of the ways institutions are rewarded and funded in order to achieve the needed change.

The perceived need for fundamental change begs the question of how such change is to be achieved. Concerns for higher education access and equity are not new. To the contrary, those notions have been with us since the Civil Rights Era of the 1960s. In spite of that, while educational attainment rates among African American, Hispanic, and economically disadvantaged students have increased modestly, they lag behind those of white students to an increasing extent (Mortensen 2006, 2007). Thus, we find ourselves not only with the same imperative to address access and equity issues, but now we must do so in an even more complex environment, punctuated by greater socioeconomic gaps in the American population, mission overlap among sectors of higher education, continued financial constraints, and a muddled public policy landscape.

Ultimately, changes will be required on a number of fronts. Public policy will need to once again support education as a public good with increased public fund-ing. States will need to rethink their goals for the institutions they oversee and adjust reward and funding mechanisms accordingly. Perhaps most importantly, a new level of leadership will need to be exhibited at the institutional level, renewing commitments to distinctive missions and fulfilling those missions in ways that are increasingly student-centric—taking into account the needs of all students within the institution's geographic reach.

This book posits that strategic enrollment management provides a unique con-ceptual framework for meeting today's challenges at the institutional level. To the SEM Planning Model, enrollment practitioners are called upon to move beyond a traditional focus on admission, marketing, and financial aid. They must be advo-cates of student access and success, creating new pathways for students to achieve their educational goals. Purveyors of SEM must also be active partners in strategic institutional planning, helping to set and adhere to priorities, and enable more effective budget planning at the institutional level.

The SEM Planning Model described in Chapter 5 provides a roadmap for moving forward with such an approach, but it is not a panacea. Institutions that attempt to implement the model in silver bullet fashion—as an isolated initiative that is deployed outside core planning and operational structures—will experience diminished results that are short-lived. Rather, effective implementation of the model requires precisely the type of fundamental restructuring called for by many in the higher education community. Effective implementation of the SEM Planning Model occurs in a context characterized by:

- Ownership from the institutions' top-level decision-making group (*i.e.*, the presidents'/chancellors' cabinet or equivalent group)
- Commitment to addressing foundational aspects of the model
  - ▶ This may involve campus conversations to gain clarity and focus of institutional mission, as well as the crafting of detailed enrollment targets. A SEM planning group will usually be charged with creating drafts and facilitating conversations. But the SEM planning group cannot make mission and enrollment goal decisions. The institutions' top-level decision-making group must be prepared to actively endorse the planning process and campus conversations, and ultimately sign off on the final products.
- Integration of the model with the core planning and operational structures of the institution, including institution-wide planning activities as well as those occurring at the college and/or departmental levels

It is a paradox of higher education in the U.S. that the very postsecondary institutions that are charged with the creation of new knowledge are so reticent to adopt new ways of doing business. Those of us who have worked within higher education often lament our slowness to change. When faced with undesirable outcomes, we are prone to make excuses and then redeploy the same tactics and strategies that failed in the past. But the time for inaction, or relying on rehashed strategies that previously fell short, has long since passed.

Whether or not strategic enrollment management truly offers an avenue for meaningful change in support of higher education's access and equity agenda remains to be seen. What is abundantly clear and within our purview as higher education professionals is our collective need to exert a new level of leadership, to identify and deploy innovative strategies that create avenues for all members of society to achieve their educational goals.

# References

ACE. *See* American Council on Education.

Advisory Committee on Student Financial Assistance. 2001. *Access Denied* [Electronic Version]. Retrieved September 22, 2007 from: <www.ed.gov/about/bdscomm/list/acsfa/access_denied.pdf>.

American Council on Education. 2006. *Students on the Move: The Future of International Students in the United States.* ACE Issue Brief [Electronic Version]. Retrieved September 16, 2007 from: <www.acenet.edu/AM/Template.cfm?Section=InfoCenter&CONTENTID=18573&TEMPLATE=/CM/Content-Display.cfm>.

Bailey, T., D. Jenkins, and T. Leinbach. 2005. Graduation rates, student goals, and measuring community college effectiveness. *Community College Research Brief.* 28 (September): 1–4. Retrieved October 14, 2007 from <ccrc.tc.columbia.edu/Publication.asp?UID=336>.

Baum, S., and L. Lapovsky. 2006. *Tuition Discounting: Not Just a Private College Practice* [Electronic Version]. New York: The College Board. Retrieved September 17, 2007 from: <www.collegeboard.com/prod_down-loads/press/tuition-discounting.pdf>.

Boehner, J.A., and H.P. McKeon. 2003. *The College Cost Crisis: A Congressional Analysis of College Costs and Implications for America's Higher Education System.* Washington, D.C.: U.S. House of Representatives, Committee on Education and the Workforce. Available at: <http://eric.ed.gov/ERICWebPortal/content-delivery/servlet/ERICServlet?accno=ED479752>.

Bontrager, B. 2004. Enrollment management: An introduction to concepts and structures. *College and University.* 79(3): 11–16.

———. 2007. The brave new world of strategic enrollment management. *College and University.* 82(2): 3–6.

Bowen, W.G. 1967. *The Economics of the Major Private Research Universities.* Berkeley CA: Carnegie Commission on Higher Education.

Breneman, D., B. Pusser, and S.E. Turner. 2006. *Earnings from Learning: The Rise of For-Profit Universities.* Albany, NY: State University of New York Press.

Breneman, D.W. 1994. *Liberal Arts Colleges: Thriving, Surviving, or Endangered?* Washington, D.C.: Brookings Institution.

Brittan, G.G., Jr. 2003. Public goods, private benefits, and the university. *The Montana Professor.* 13(1): 3–7.

Brown, G. 2005. *A Budgetary Perspective on Strategic Enrollment Management: Shaping the Financial Future.* AACRAO Annual Meeting pre-conference workshop. Boston.

Copeland, T., and A. Wells. 2008. *Enabling SEM: Linking Planning and Performance.* Unpublished paper, SunGard Higher Education.

Davis, J.S. 2003. Unintended consequences of tuition discounting. *Lumina Foundation for Education New Agenda Series.* 5(1): 1–33. Retrieved August 4, 2008 from: <www.luminafoundation.org/publications/Tuitiondiscounting.pdf>.

Dickeson, R.C. 2004. *Collision Course: Rising College Costs Threaten America's Future and Require Shared Solutions.* Indianapolis, IN: Lumina Foundation for Education. Available at: <http://eric.ed.gov/ERICWebPortal/contentdelivery/servlet/ERICServlet?accno=ED497036>.

Dill, D.D. 2003. An institutional perspective on higher education policy: The case of academic quality assurance. In *Higher Education: Handbook of Theory and Research (Vol. XVIII),* edited by J. Smart. Dordrecht, Netherlands: Kluwer. Retrieved August 4, 2008 from: <www.utwente.nl/cheps/documenten/SusuDill.pdf>.

Dolence, M.G. 1993. *Strategic Enrollment Management: A Primer for Campus Administrators*. Washington, D.C.: American Association of Collegiate Registrars and Admissions Officers.

———. 1995. *Strategic Enrollment Management : Cases from the Field*. Washington, D.C.: American Association of Collegiate Registrars and Admissions Officers.

Doyle, W.R. 2006. Community college transfers and college graduation: Whose choices matter most? *Change*. 38(3): 56–58. Retrieved July 10, 2008 from: <www.carnegiefoundation.org/change/sub.asp?key=98&subkey=1711>.

Driscoll, A.K. 2007. *Beyond Access: How the First Semester Matters for Community College Students' Aspirations and Persistence*. Retrieved July 10, 2008 from: <pace.berkeley.edu/reports/PB.07–2.pdf>.

Ehrehberg, R.G. 2006. *Tuition Rising: Why College Costs So Much*. Cambridge, MA: Harvard University Press.

Fliegler, C.M. 2006. 'Mission creep' or mission possible? *University Business*. March. Retrieved May 14, 2008 from: <www.universitybusiness.com/ViewArticle.aspx?articleid=70>.

Green, T. 2005. Financial aid, access, and America's social contract with higher education. *College and University*. (80)3: 9–13.

Harvey, J. 1998. *Straight Talk About College Costs and Prices: Report of the National Commission on the Cost of Higher Education*. Phoenix, AZ: Oryx Press.

Haycock, K. 2006. *Promise Abandoned: How Policy Choices and Institutional Practices Restrict College Opportunities*. Washington, D.C.: The Education Trust.

Hebel, S. 2006. Tuition: Some increases slow down, but concerns linger. *The Chronicle of Higher Education*. 52(18). Retrieved September 16, 2007 from: <http://chronicle.com/weekly/v52/i18/18a01201.htm>.

Heller, D.E. 2001. *The States and Public Higher Education Policy: Affordability, Access, and Accountability*. Baltimore and London: The Johns Hopkins University Press.

Henderson, S.E. 2001. On the brink of a profession. In *The SEM Revolution*, edited by J. Black. Washington, D.C.: American Association of Collegiate Registrars and Admissions Officers.

Hoover, E. 2007. Hoping to attract more middle-income students, Amherst College replaces loans with grants. *The Chronicle of Higher Education*. Retrieved September, 20, 2007 from <http://chronicle.com/daily/2007/07/2007072003n.htm>.

Hossler, D. 1984. *Enrollment Management: An Integrated Approach*. New York: The College Board.

———. 2004. Refinancing public universities: Student enrollments, incentive-based budgeting, and incremental revenue. In *Public Funding of Higher Education*, edited by E.P. St. John and M.D. Parsons. Baltimore, MD: Johns Hopkins University Press.

———. 2006. Anticipating the future of college admissions. *The College Board Review*.

———. 2007. Un-complicating community college transfer. Retrieved September, 14, 2007 from: <www.insidehighered.com/news/2007/09/14/newjersey>. *Inside Higher Ed*.

Hossler, D., J. Bean, and Associates. 1990. *The Strategic Management of College Enrollments*. San Francisco: Jossey-Bass..

Kalsbeek, D. 2005. *The Challenge of Access: Structures, Strategies, and SEM Antics*. Presentation at the AACRAO Strategic Enrollment Management Conference, Chicago, IL, 2005.

———. 2006. Some reflections on SEM structures and strategies (part 1). *College and University*. 81(3): 3–10.

Lederman, D. 2008. Conceiving a new agenda for public higher education. *Inside Higher Ed*. June 10. Retrieved June 17, 2008 from: <www.insidehighered.com/news/2008/06/10/publics>.

Lewis, L. 2007. Florida universities brace for budget cuts. *The Chronicle of Higher Education*. 53(47). Retrieved September 15, 2007 from: <http://chronicle.com/weekly/v53/i47/47a01801.htm>.

Maguire, J. 1976. To the organized go the students. *Bridge Magazine* (Boston College alumni magazine). XXXIX(i).

Marklein, M.B. 2004. Low-income students scarce at elite colleges. *USA Today*. September 20. Retrieved September 29, 2007 from: <www.usatoday.com/news/nation/2004–09–20-cover-colleges_x.htm>.

Middaugh, M.F. 2005. Understanding higher education costs. *Planning for Higher Education*. 33(3): 5–18.

Mortensen, T. 2006. Family income and higher education opportunity, 1970–2003. *Postsecondary Education Opportunity*. 174(December): 1–11.